A pattern language
for web usability

A pattern language for web usability

Ian Graham

ADDISON-WESLEY

An imprint of **Pearson Education**

London ◆ Boston ◆ Indianapolis ◆ New York ◆ Mexico City ◆ Toronto ◆ Sydney ◆ Tokyo ◆ Singapore
Hong Kong ◆ Cape Town ◆ New Delhi ◆ Madrid ◆ Paris ◆ Amsterdam ◆ Munich ◆ Milan ◆ Stockholm

PEARSON EDUCATION LIMITED

Head Office
Edinburgh Gate
Harlow CM20 2JE
Tel: +44 (0)1279 623623
Fax: +44 (0)1279 431059

London Office:
128 Long Acre, London WC2E 9AN
Tel: +44 (0)20 7447 2000
Fax: +44 (0)20 7447 2170
www.it-minds.com
www.awprofessional.com

First published in Great Britain in 2003
© Pearson Education Limited 2003

The right of Ian Graham to be identified as author of this work has been asserted by him in
accordance with the Copyright, Designs and Patents Act 1988.

ISBN 0 201 78888 8

British Library Cataloguing in Publication Data
A CIP catalog record for this book can be obtained from the British Library

Library of Congress Cataloging-in-Publication Data
Graham, Ian
    A pattern language of Web usability/Ian Graham.
      p. cm.
    Includes bibliographical references and index.
    ISBN 0-201-78888-8 (pbk. :alk. paper)
    1. Web sites--Design. 2. Example. I. Title.

TK5105.888 .G69 2003
005.7'2--dc21

2002034460

10 9 8 7 6 5 4 3 2 1

Typeset by Pantek Arts Ltd, Maidstone, Kent.
Printed and bound in Italy by Rotolito Lombarda.

The publishers' policy is to use paper manufactured from sustainable forests.

Contents

Trademark notice

Preface

During the second half of the 1990s software developers were influenced hugely by the work of architectural theorists of the built environment, notably Christopher Alexander and his colleagues. Alexander's idea of a pattern language for planning, designing and constructing towns and buildings was taken as the inspiration for catalogs of software design patterns and programming language idioms. In a more recent development, some software engineers have gone back to Alexander's work and realized that pattern catalogs miss the essence of the idea: that the 'words' in a language can be combined using its grammar to produce beautiful, useful works. Natural language users make exquisite prose or poetry; pattern language users should therefore be able to produce great software. Examples of such languages, in the context of software development, include Jim Coplien's organizational pattern language and Alan O'Callaghan's ADAPTOR language for technology adoption and migration.

The second notable development of that half-decade was the emergence into ubiquity of the world wide web. Despite the astronomical number of hours invested in developing websites for commercial and other uses, it is quite clear that the vast majority of these sites are effectively unusable and the first dot coms have already bitten the dust as a result. One reason for this is that the new generation of web designers seems to be ignorant of 20 years of R&D into human computer interaction and graphical user interface design. One possible solution to the problem is a pattern language for designing usable websites.

There are a few good books on web design, most notably the ones by Jakob Nielsen. However, the wisdom in these books is not organized in such a way that it can be accessed quickly as a reference guide to good practice. Secondly, many of the principles of good user interface design, and *a fortiori* an understanding of the insights of cognitive psychology that underpins them, are only present implicitly in these books. Therefore, a standard reference pattern language would be a useful reference and a source of learning on how to design great sites.

There are four aspects of website design: usability, content, navigation and aesthetics. The last three all contribute in some way to the first. Therefore the language must address all four issues. The web usability (*wu*) pattern language presented in this work attempts to meet these requirements.

There is little original in this book, most of the ideas having been published elsewhere already. This is as it should be in a book of patterns because patterns should represent recognizable, well-known solutions to recurring problems. What we offer in place of originality is a handy reference to existing best practice, organized in a way that reflects the structure of a typical web design project.

The author's expectation is that the publication of a first edition of the language will generate feedback leading to a possible revision and expansion based on concrete experiences (of both success and failure, of course).

Who should read this book?

This book is intended as a practical guide for web designers and managers of website development projects. It should be used as a simple checklist as these people go through the design process. It will also be of interest to people interested in web design and summarizes much of what can be found in the several other books on the subject. The patterns and human–computer interaction (HCI) communities may be interested for their own respective reasons. Researchers in the area and students may also gain from reading it.

How to read this book

Chapter 1 presents a perhaps rather academic introduction to patterns in general. Readers who are already familiar with patterns and, most importantly, with the distinction between a pattern language and a pattern catalog may skim through this chapter very quickly. Some may wish to skip directly to section 1.5, which discusses the above distinction.

Chapter 2 starts by providing motivation for the author's need to create this book and then discusses usability in general with only a few references to issues specific to the web. Again, after the opening remarks, most of it may be skimmed or even skipped altogether by readers with some background in HCI.

Chapter 3 motivates and presents the pattern language itself. There are 79 patterns, grouped into four sections. Each section starts with a diagram showing how the patterns link together. Since navigating amongst them may be a tad tedious, as one must follow the pointers in each pattern and flick to different pages, we have provided a website containing a hypertext version of the patterns. The intention, however, is that the chapter should be read sequentially at first reading. Then the interested reader can go to the website to get a feeling for the navigation. One advantage of this is that the author will be able to update the patterns on the web as he discovers more about them, and as they are ground finer through the mills of various pattern writer's workshops. Chapter 3 gives more information on how to access and use the site.

Chapter 4 gives a few examples of how to select patterns and guidelines as to how apply them to actual design projects.

The reader who wishes only to see a discussion of web-related issues may confidently start reading at Chapter 3 and perhaps return to the first two chapters later for the background they provide.

Lastly, this book is not to be read as a critique of particular websites. Where we have included images of websites it is usually to show how well they implement a particular pattern rather than to criticise them.

The origins of *wu* This pattern language originated when the author organized a workshop at the OT2001 conference in Oxford, England. He suggested the names and outlines of about 70 patterns based on his own work (Graham, 2001) and other references, notably Nielsen (2000) and Spool *et al.* (1999). These references were made available to participants during the workshop, so that they could get more detail on patterns that had been inspired by these books.

Everyone was given a hard copy of a list consisting of just the names and, in some cases, very brief descriptions of the putative patterns and a bunch of copies of a blank pattern pro forma. They were asked to choose the pattern(s) they had an opinion about or interest in from this list, and find the pro forma(s) to go with them. They then had to 'fight' for the filled-in forms for the patterns they chose to work on, on a first-come-first-served basis. Participants worked in pairs but these pairs often interacted with each other. They added new patterns using blank pro formas. People were asked to classify their patterns and, especially, to note any related patterns. Could these patterns form sequences in the language with respect to some particular web design problem? One pair, for example, focused on workflow-oriented sites. A few completely new patterns emerged and we found some overlap among the starting set. Ian Graham then undertook to write up the work done and publish it on the www.trireme.com site for discussion among the group and comment by other interested parties. It was suggested that the material would appear in book form when it had assumed some degree of completeness. This book is the result.

As a result of the origins of *wu,* the author's opinions are often expressed in the first person plural. This is not the royal 'we' by any means; it expresses his humility in the face of the realization of how few of these ideas are original. Rather, it represents the 'we' of collective ownership and origin. Sometimes, but seldom, it represents the view of Trireme International, e.g. when talking about the *wu* website. Of course, he also uses the 'conspiratorial' we to convey a shared understanding or effort by reader and author.

And while we are on the subject of grammar, the word 'he' does not imply any assumption about sexual gender.

Acknowledgments   Those in attendance at the original workshop, for all or part of the session, were Richard Dué (Thomsen Dué and Associates Ltd, Canada), Paul Dyson (England), Ian Graham (Trireme International, England), Andy Harbach (SecureTrading, Wales), Kevlin Henney (Curbralan, England), Mattias Larsson (Sweden), Mary Lynn Manns (University of North Carolina, USA), Sabah Mehrad (Trireme International, England), Linda Rising (USA), Chris Simons (Princeton Softech, England), Dave Sissons (Royal Sun Alliance, England), Gareth Sylvester-Bradley (England), Jari Worsley (Hyperlink, England) and Detlef Vollmann (Switzerland). My thanks to all their contributions, which are acknowledged pattern by pattern.

Four of the patterns were subjected to a rigorous critique at EuroPLop 2002 (Graham, 2002) and I thank Frank Buschmann, Kevlin Henney, Nora Koch, Oliver Vogel and Uwe Zdun for all their helpful advice.

I would also like to thank the authors of the other books and websites concerned with web usability that I have had the privilege of consulting and borrowing ideas from. Significant influence is also acknowledged against each pattern. Thanks to my publishers for all their help and assistance during the production of this book – and for bullying me into finishing the manuscript.

Alan O'Callaghan wrote a good number of the words in Chapter 1, so I would like to thank him especially.

Ian Graham
London, 2002

We are grateful to the following for permission to reproduce copyright material:

Pattern 3 image © 2002 Banco de México Diego Rivera & Frida Kahlo Museums Trust. Av. Cinco de Mayo No. 2, Col. Centro, Del. Cuauhtémoc 06059, México, D. F.; Patterns 6 and 56 images reproduced courtesy of Dorling Kindersley Ltd; Pattern 37 reproduced courtesy of Dorling Kindersley Ltd and Guy Ryecart; Pattern 74 reproduced courtesy of Dorling Kindersley Ltd and by kind permission of the Trustees of the Imperial War Museum, London; Pattern 10 and Figure 3.7 screenshots Netscape website © 2002 Netscape Communications Corporation. Screenshots used with permission; Pattern 13 screenshot © Crown copyright material is reproduced with the permission of the Controller of HMSO and Queen's Printer for Scotland; Pattern 16 image copyright Tate London 2002. The work illustrated on page 113 has been reproduced by permission of the Henry Moore Foundation; Patterns 17 and 35 screenshots reprinted by permission from Microsoft Corporation; Pattern 23 screenshot Jakob Nielsen; Pattern 25 screenshot (top) Amazon.de GmbH; Pattern 28 screenshot David Gordon and Colin Craven; Pattern 47 screenshot Financial Times; Pattern 50 screenshot VWR International, VWRI chromatography website www.chromatography.co.uk; Pattern 51 image © Crown copyright. Reproduced with the permission of the Controller of HMSO and the Queen's Printer for Scotland; Pattern 60 and Figure 3.17 screenshots Derek M. Powazek; Pattern 61 cartoon Dave Lochner; Pattern 62 screenshot reproduced with the permission of AltaVista Internet Operations Limited. All rights reserved; Pattern 72 screenshot reproduced by permission of VeriSign, Inc; Pattern 78 image Advanced Drainage Systems, Inc.

Abridged extracts from *A Pattern Language* by Christopher Alexander, copyright 1977 by Christopher Alexander. Used by permission of Oxford University Press, Inc.

In some instances we have been unable to trace the owners of copyright material, and we would appreciate any information that would enable us to do so.

1 An introduction to patterns

with Alan O'Callaghan

Thou cunning'st pattern of excelling nature
W. Shakespeare, *Othello*

This chapter provides an introduction to the concepts of patterns and pattern languages. It provides important background information to other chapters. The reader is advised to read the section of the Preface entitled 'How to read this book' before continuing.

1.1 What are patterns?

One of the most important recent ideas in software development is that of a design pattern. Design patterns are standard solutions to recurring problems, named to help people discuss them easily and to think about design. They have always been around in computing, so that terms such as 'linked list' or 'recursive descent' are readily understood by people in the field.

Software patterns have been described as reusable micro-architectures. Patterns are abstract, core solutions to problems that recur in different contexts but encounter the same 'forces' each time. The actual implementation of the solution varies with each application. Patterns are not, therefore, ready-made 'pluggable' solutions. They are most often represented in object-oriented development by commonly recurring arrangements of classes and the structural and dynamic connections between them. Perhaps the best known and useful examples of patterns occur in application frameworks associated with graphical user interface (GUI) building or other well-defined development problems. In fact, some of the motivation for the patterns movement came from the apprehension of already existing frameworks that led people to wonder how general the approach was. Nowadays it is more usual to deliver frameworks in the form of flexible class libraries for use by programmers in languages that support the class concept, often C++ and Java. Examples of frameworks range from class libraries that are delivered with programming environments through the NeXtStep Interface Builder to the many GUI and client–server development systems now on the market, and such as Delphi, Visual Studio, Visual Age and Visual Basic.

Victorian builders used huge pattern books to design houses with their clients. The book contained pictures of ornarmented windows, doors, cornices, fireplaces and other architectural features. They would go through these illustrations selecting the styles and discussing the consistency of their choices. The result is a surprisingly wide-ranging stock of Victorian housing, much of which is pleasant to inhabit to this day.

Patterns today are most useful because they provide a language for designers to communicate in. Rather than having to explain a complex idea from scratch, the designer can just mention a pattern by name and everyone will know, at least roughly, what is meant. This is how designers in many other disciplines communicate their design ideas. In this sense they are an excellent vehicle for the collection and dissemination of the anecdotal and unquantifiable data that Borenstein (1991) argues need to be collected before we can see real advances in the processes of building software. There are two different views of patterns abroad, both of which have value. To examine these we will first look at the roots of the patterns concept that lie outside the domain of software development, in the domain of the built environment. Patterns are closely related to software architecture.

Patterns are associated with the radical architect of the built environment, Christopher Alexander. From the outset of his career

Alexander has been driven by the view that the vast majority of building stock created since the end of World War II (which constitutes the great majority of all construction works created by human beings in the history of the species) has been dehumanizing, of poor quality and lacking all sense of beauty and human feeling. In his earliest publication Alexander presented a powerful critique of modern design (Alexander, 1964) contrasting the failures of the professional *self-conscious* process of design with what he called the *unselfconscious* process by which peasants' farmhouses, Eskimos' igloos and the huts of the Mousgoum tribesmen of the Cameroon amongst others create their living spaces. In the latter '... the pattern of building operation, the pattern of the building's maintenance, the constraints of the surrounding conditions, and also the pattern of daily life, are fused in the form ...' (p. 31) yet there is no concept of 'design' or 'architecture', let alone separate designers and architects. Each man builds his own house.

Alexander argues that the unselfconscious process has a homeostatic (i.e. self-organizing) structure that produces well-fitting forms even in the face of change, but in the self-conscious process this homeostatic structure has been broken down, making poorly-fitting forms almost inevitable.[1] Although, by definition, there are no explicitly articulated rules for building in the unselfconscious process, there is usually a great weight of unspoken, unwritten, implicit rules that are, nevertheless, rigidly maintained by culture and tradition. These traditions provide a bedrock of stability, but more than that, a viscosity or resistance to all but the most urgent changes – usually when a form 'fails' in some way. When such changes are required, the very simplicity of life itself, and the immediacy of the feedback (since the builder and homeowner are

---

[1] Mature biological systems are homeostatic. Consider how a tree, for example a mighty oak in a wood, is formed. The shape of an individual tree appears well adapted to its environment. The height of the tree is a factor of its competition with neighbouring trees. If used as a windbreak on the edges of farms, it will typically be bent in the direction of the prevailing wind patterns. The number of branches it has depends on the number of leaves it produces to accommodate local sunshine and rainfall conditions, etc. If alone on a hilltop, the pattern of growth is normally symmetrical, but if constrained in any way, the tree reflects the constraints in its own growth pattern. The tree's adaptiveness is, of course, a function of its genetic code. More recently Alexander has talked of his own approach as being a 'genetic' approach and the job of patterns is to instil this genetic code into structures.

one and the same), mean that the necessary adaptation can itself be made immediately, as a 'one-off'. Thus the unselfconscious process is characterized by fast reactions to single 'failures' combined with resistance to all other changes. This allows the process to make a series of minor, incremental adjustments instead of spasmodic, global ones. Changes have local impact only, and over a long period of time; the system adjusts 'subsystem by subsystem'. Since the minor changes happen at a faster rate of change than does the culture, equilibrium is constantly and dynamically re-established after each disturbance.

In the self-conscious process, tradition is weakened or becomes non-existent. The feedback loop is lengthened by the distance between the 'user' and the builder. Immediate reaction to failure is not possible because materials are not close to hand. Failures for all these reasons accumulate and require far more drastic action because they have to be dealt with in combination. All the factors that drive the construction process to equilibrium have disappeared in the self-conscious process. Equilibrium, if reached at all, is unstable, not least because the rate of cultural change outpaces the rate at which adaptations can be made.

Alexander does not seek a return to primitive forms, but rather a new approach to a modern dilemma: self-conscious designers, and indeed the notion of design itself, have arisen as a result of the increased complexity of requirements and sophistication of materials. They now have control over the process to a degree that the unselfconscious craftsman never had. But the more control they get, the greater the cognitive burden and the greater the effort they spend in trying to deal with it, the more obscure becomes the causal structure of the problem that needs to be expressed for a well-fitting solution to be created. Increasingly, the very individuality of the designer is turning into its opposite: instead of being a solution, it is the main obstacle to a solution to the problem of restoring equilibrium between form and context.

In his 1964 work, Alexander produced a semi-algorithmic, mechanistic 'programme' based on functional decomposition (supported by a mathematical description in an appendix) to address the issues he identified. He has long since abandoned that prescription. It is the rather more informal drawings he used in his worked examples that seem to have a more lasting significance. These became the basis, it seems, for the patterns in his later work.

Alexandrian 'theory' is currently expressed in an 11-volume-strong literary project that does not include his 1964 work. Eight of these volumes have been published so far (though, at best, three of them, referred to as the patterns trilogy, *The Timeless Way of Building*, *A Pattern Language* and *The Oregon Experiment*, are familiar to parts of the software patterns movement).[2] The ninth volume in the series, *The Nature of Order,* is eagerly awaited as it promises to provide the fullest exposition yet of the underlying theory. A common theme of all the books is the rejection of abstract categories of architectural or design principles as being entirely arbitrary. Also rejected is the idea that it is even possible to design successfully 'very abstract forms at the big level' (Alexander, 1996, p.8). For Alexander, architecture attains its highest expression not at the level of gross structure, but actually in its finest detail: what he calls 'fine structure'. That is to say, the macroscopic clarity of design comes from a consistency; a geometric unity holds true at all levels of scale. It is not possible for a single mind to imagine this recursive structure at all levels in advance of building it. It is in this context that his patterns for the built environment must be understood.

Alexander *et al.* (1977) present an archetypal pattern language for construction. The language is an interconnected network of 253 patterns that encapsulate design best practice at a variety of levels of scale, from the siting of alcoves to the construction of towns and cities. The language is designed to be used collaboratively by all the stakeholders in a development, not just developers. This is predicated, in part at least, on the assumption that the real experts in buildings are those who live and work in them rather than those who have studied architecture or structural engineering formally. The patterns are applied to the construction itself sequentially. Each

---

[2] These three books, along with *The Linz Café, The Production of Houses, A New Theory of Urban Design, A Foreshadowing of 21st Century Art* and *The Mary Rose Museum*, are published by Oxford University Press. In preparation are *The Nature of Order, Sketches of a New Architecture* and *Battle: The Story of an Historic Clash Between World System A and World System B.*

state change caused by the application of a pattern creates a new context to which the next pattern can be applied. The overall development is an emergent property of the application of the pattern language. The language therefore has a generative character: it generates solutions piecemeal from the successive addressing of each individual problem that each of the patterns addresses separately.

WAIST-HIGH SHELF (pattern number 201 in the language) proposes the building of waist-high shelves around main rooms to hold the 'traffic' of objects that are handled most, so that they are always ready to hand. Clearly the specific form, depth, position and so on of these shelves will differ from house to house and workplace to workplace. The implementation of the pattern creates, therefore, a very specific context in which other patterns, such as **THICKENING THE OUTER WALL** (number 211), can be used since Alexander suggests the shelves be built into the very structure of the building where appropriate, and using **THINGS FROM YOUR LIFE** (number 253) to populate the shelves.

The pattern that more than any other is the physical and procedural embodiment of Alexander's approach to design, however, is pattern number 208, **GRADUAL STIFFENING**:

The fundamental philosophy behind the use of pattern languages is that buildings should be uniquely adapted to individual needs and sites; and that the plans of buildings should be rather loose and fluid, in order to accommodate these subtleties ...

Recognize that you are not assembling a building from components like an erector set, but that you are instead weaving a structure which starts out globally complete, but flimsy; then gradually making it stiffer but still rather flimsy; and only finally making it completely stiff and strong.

(Alexander *et al.*, 1977, pp. 963–9.)

In the description of this pattern Alexander invites the reader to visualize a 50-year-old master carpenter at work. He keeps working, apparently without stopping, until he eventually produces a quality product. The smoothness of his labor comes from the fact that he is making small, sequential, incremental steps such that he can always eliminate a mistake or correct an imperfection with the next step. He compares this with the novice who, with a 'panic-stricken attention to detail', tries to work out everything in advance, fearful of making an unrecoverable error. Alexander's point is that most modern architecture has the character of the novice's work, not the master craftsman's. Successful construction processes, producing well-fitting forms, come from the postponement of detailed design decisions until the building process itself so that the details are fitted into the overall, evolving structure.

1.2 Patterns in software engineering

Alexander's ideas seem to have been first introduced into the software community by Kent Beck and Ward Cunningham. In a 1993 article in *Smalltalk Report*, Beck claimed to have been using patterns for six years already, but the software patterns movement seems to have been kicked off by a workshop on the production of a software architect's handbook organized by Bruce Anderson for OOPSLA '91. Here met for the first time Erich Gamma, Richard Helm, Ralph Johnson and John Vlissides – a group destined to gain notoriety as the Gang of Four (GoF). Gamma was already near to completion of his PhD thesis on design patterns in the ET++ framework. He had already been joined by Helm in the production of an independent catalogue. By the time of a follow-up meeting at OOPSLA in 1992, first Vlissides and then Johnson had joined the effort and, some time in 1993, the group agreed to write a book that has been a best-seller ever since its publication in 1995. In fact, outside the patterns movement itself, many in the software development industry identify software patterns completely and totally with the GoF book.

However, the 1991 OOPSLA workshop was only the first in a series of meetings that culminated first in the formation of the non-profit Hillside Group[3] (apparently so-called because they went off

---

[3] The founding members were Ken Auer, Kent Beck, Grady Booch, Jim Coplien, Ward Cunningham, Hal Hildebrand and Ralph Johnson. The initial sponsors were Rational and the Object Management Group.

to a hillside one weekend to try out Alexander's building patterns) and then the first Pattern Languages of Programming (PLoP) conference in 1994. PLoP conferences, organized and funded by the Hillside Group, take place in America, Germany and Australia annually. Collections of the patterns that are produced are published in a series by Addison-Wesley. In addition, the Hillside Group maintains a website and numerous pattern mailing lists. These communication channels form the backbone of a large and growing community known as the patterns movement.

A characteristic of the way in which patterns are developed for publication in the patterns movement is the so-called pattern writers' workshop. This is a form of peer review that is loosely related to design reviews that are typical in software development processes, but more strongly related to poetry circles, which are decidedly atypical. The special rules of the pattern writers' workshop (which are the modus operandi of the PLoP conferences) have been shown to be powerful in producing software patterns, written in easily accessible, regular forms known as **pattern templates**, at an appropriate level of abstraction. Rising (1998) reports on their effectiveness in producing a patterns culture in the telecommunications company AGCS; and they are de rigueur in parts of IBM, Siemens and AT&T, all of which are known to have produced their own in-house software patterns, as well as publishing them in the public domain.

While the GoF book has won deserved recognition for raising the profile of patterns, for many it has been a double-edged sword. The GoF patterns form a catalog of stand-alone patterns all at a similar level of abstraction. Such a catalog can never have the generative quality that Alexander's pattern language claims for itself and, to be fair, the Gang of Four freely admits that this was not the aim of their work.

The GoF book includes 23 useful design patterns, including the following particularly interesting and useful ones:

◆ **FAÇADE** Useful for implementing object wrappers: combines multiple interfaces into one.

◆ **ADAPTER** Also useful for wrappers: converts interfaces into ones that are understandable by clients.

◆ **PROXY** Mainly used to support distribution: creates a local surrogate for a remote object to enable access to it.

◆ **OBSERVER** Helps an object to notify registrants that its state has changed and helps with the implementation of blackboard systems.

◆ **VISITOR AND STATE** These two patterns help to implement dynamic classification.

◆ **COMPOSITE** Allows clients to treat parts and wholes uniformly.

◆ **BRIDGE** Helps with decoupling interfaces from their implementations.

Some cynics claim that some of the GoF patterns are really only useful for fixing deficiencies in the C++ language. Examples of these might arguably include **DECORATOR** and **ITERATOR**. However, this very suggestion raises the issue of language-dependent versus language-independent patterns. Buschmann *et al.* (1996) (also known as the Party of Five or PoV) from Siemens in Germany suggest a system of patterns that can be divided into architectural patterns, design patterns and language idioms. They present examples of the first two categories. Architectural patterns include **PIPES AND FILTERS, BLACKBOARD** systems, and the **MODEL VIEW CONTROLLER** (MVC) pattern for user interface development. Typical PoV design patterns are called:

◆ **FORWARDER RECEIVER**

◆ **WHOLE-PART**

◆ **PROXY**.

The reader is advised by the PoV to refer to all the GoF patterns as well. The PoV book can therefore be regarded as an expansion of the original catalogue, not merely through the addition of extra patterns, but by addressing different levels of abstraction too. The **WHOLE-PART** pattern is exactly the implementation of the composition structures that form part of basic object modeling semantics. In that sense it appears to be a trivial pattern. However, since most languages do not support the construct, it can be useful to see the standard way to implement it. It is a rare example of an analysis pattern that maps directly to an idiom in several languages: a multi-language idiom. The best known source of idiomatic (i.e. language-specific) patterns is Jim Coplien's book on advanced C++, which predates the GoF book by some three years (Coplien, 1992). C++ 'patterns' (the book does not use the term) that Coplien presents include:

◆ **HANDLE CLASS**, used to encapsulate classes that bear application intelligence;

◆ **REFERENCE COUNTER**, managing a reference count to shared representation;

◆ **ENVELOPE-LETTER** permits 'type migration' of classes;

◆ **EXEMPLAR** enables the creation of prototypes in the absence of delegation;

◆ **AMBASSADOR** provides distribution transparency.

Whilst experienced object-oriented programmers will feel immediately familiar with many of these patterns, almost everyone will recognize the ideas behind caches and recursive composites. These too can be regarded as design and/or analysis patterns. **CACHE** should be used when complex computations make it better to store the results rather than recalculate often; or when the cost of bringing data across a network makes it more efficient to store them locally. Clearly this is a pattern having much to do with performance optimization. It is also worth noting that patterns may use each other; this pattern may make use of the **OBSERVER** pattern when it is necessary to know that the results need to be recalculated or the data refreshed.

The above examples indicate that a standard pattern layout may be beneficial, and many proponents adopt a standard based loosely on Alexander's work: the so-called Alexandrian form. This divides pattern descriptions into prose sections with suitable pictorial illustrations as follows – although the actual headings vary from author to author:

◆ Pattern name and description.

◆ Context (problem) – situations where the patterns may be useful and the problem that the pattern solves.

◆ Forces – the contradictory forces at work that the designer must balance.

◆ Solution – the principles underlying the pattern and how to apply it (including examples of its realization, consequences and benefits).

◆ Also Known As/Related patterns – other names for (almost) the same thing and patterns that this one uses or might occur with.

◆ Known uses.

Actually, this deviates quite a lot from Alexander's presentation, as we shall see later.

Kent Beck has produced a book of 92 Smalltalk idioms (Beck, 1997) and there have been a number of language-specific 'versions' of the GoF book, notably for Smalltalk (Alpert *et al.*, 1998) and Java (Grand, 1998; Cooper, 2000). Although many of the PoV architectural patterns exist also among the Software Engineering Institute's (SEI, Carnegie Mellon University) 'styles', it is crucial to note their different purposes. Both are abstracted from software development best practice, but by the SEI in order to collect and formalize (and presumably later automate) them, and by the PoV in order to further generalize that practice.

The overwhelming majority of software patterns produced to date have been design patterns at various levels of abstraction, but Coad (1992), Coad *et al.* (1997) and Fowler (1997) introduced the idea of analysis patterns as opposed to design patterns. Fowler's patterns are reusable fragments of object-oriented specification models made generic enough to be applicable across a number of specific application domains. They therefore have something of the flavour of the GoF pattern catalog (described in that book's subtitle as 'elements of reusable object-oriented software') but are even further removed from Alexander's generative concepts. Examples of Fowler's patterns include:

◆ **PARTY:** how to store the name and address of someone or something you deal with.

◆ **ORGANIZATION STRUCTURE:** how to represent divisional structure.

◆ **POSTING RULES:** how to represent basic bookkeeping rules.

◆ **QUOTE:** dealing with the different ways in which financial instrument prices are represented.

There are many more, some specialized into domains such as health or accounting.

The problem with these patterns is that even the simplest ones – like **ACCOUNTABILITY** – are really quite hard to understand compared with the difficulty of the underlying problem that they solve. The present author had three goes at reading the text before really understanding what was going on. At the end of this process he found that he knew the proposed solution already but would never have expressed it in the same terms.

1.3 Organizational patterns

Apart from systems development, there has also been interest in developing patterns for organizational development (Coplien, 1995; O'Callaghan, 1997a, 1997b, 1998). Coplien applies the idea of patterns to the software development process itself and observes several noteworthy regularities. These observations arose out of a research project sponsored by AT&T investigating the value of QA process standards such as ISO9001 and the SEI's Capability Maturity Model. Working from a base concept that real processes were characterized by their communication pathways, Coplien, together with Brad Cain and Neil Harrison, analyzed more than 50 projects by medium-size, high-productivity software development organizations, including the Borland team charged with developing the Quattro Pro spreadsheet product. The technique they used was to adapt Class Responsibility and Collaboration (CRC) cards and to get, in a workshop situation, representatives of the development organization under focus to enumerate roles (as opposed to job descriptions), identify and categorize the strength of the relationships between those roles (as either weak, medium and strong), and then to role-play the development process in order to validate their judgements. The information was then input into a

Smalltalk-based system called Pasteur that produces a variety of different sociometric diagrams and measures. From these, Coplien *et al.* were able to identify the commonly recurring key characteristics of the most productive organizations and develop a 42-strong pattern language to aid the design of development organizations. Included in the language are patterns such as these:

◆ **CONWAY'S LAW** states that architecture always follows organization or vice versa.

◆ **ARCHITECT ALSO IMPLEMENTS** requires that the architect stands close to the development process.

◆ **DEVELOPER CONTROLS PROCESS** requires that the developers own and drive the development process, as opposed to having one imposed on them.

◆ **MERCENARY ANALYST** enables the 'off-line' reverse engineering and production of project documentation.

◆ **FIREWALL** describes how to insulate developers from the 'white noise' of the software development industry.

◆ **GATEKEEPER** describes how to get useful information in a timely manner to software developers.

A typical application of such organizational patterns is the combined use of **GATEKEEPER** and **FIREWALL** in, say, a situation where a pilot project is assessing new technology. The software development industry excels at rumour–mongering, a situation fuelled by the practice of vendors who make vapourware announcements long in advance of any commercial-strength implementations. Overattention to the whispers on the industry grapevine, let alone authoritative-looking statements in the trade press, can seriously undermine a pilot project. Developers lose confidence in Java, say, because of its reputation for poor performance or a claimed lack of available tools. Yet, at the same time, some news is important: for example, the publication of Platform 2 for Java. A solution is to build official firewalls and then create a gatekeeper role where a nominated individual, or perhaps a virtual center such as an Object Center, is responsible for filtering and forwarding the useful and usable information as opposed to unsubstantiated scare stories, junk mail and even the attention of vendors' salesforces.

More interesting than the individual patterns themselves, however, is the underlying approach of Coplien's language, which is much closer to the spirit of Alexander's work than anything to be found in the GoF or PoV books, for example. First, since its very scope is intercommunication between people, it is human-centered. Second, it is explicitly generative in its aim. Coplien argues that while software developers do not inhabit code in the way that people inhabit houses and offices, as professionals they are expert users of professional processes and organizations. Therefore, just as Alexander's language is designed to involve all the stakeholders of building projects (and, above all, the expertise of the users of the buildings), so process designers have to base themselves on the expertise of the victims of formal processes: the developers themselves. Coplien's attempt to create an avowedly Alexandrian pattern language seems to push the focus of his patterns away from descriptions of fragments of structure (as is typical in the GoF patterns) much more towards descriptions of the work that has to be done. In going beyond mere structure, Coplien's patterns have much more of a feel of genuine architecture about them than do many other pattern types available.

In fact, it is clear that from common roots there are two polarized views of patterns abroad today. One view focuses on patterns as generic structural descriptions. They have been described, in Unified Modeling Language (UML) books especially, as 'parameterized collaborations'. The suggestion is that you can take, say, the structural descriptions of the roles that different classes can play in a pattern and then, simply by changing the class names and providing detailed algorithmic implementations, plug them into a software development. Patterns thus become reduced to abstract descriptions of potentially pluggable components. A problem with this simplistic view occurs when a single class is required to play many roles simultaneously in different patterns. Erich Gamma has recently reimplemented the HotDraw framework, for example, in Java. One class, **FIGURE**, appears to collaborate in fourteen different overlapping patterns – it is difficult to see how the design could have been successful if each of these patterns had been instantiated as a separate component. More importantly, this view has nothing to say about how software projects should be put together, only what (fragments of) it might look like structurally. The other view regards them simply as design decisions (taken in a particular context, in response to a problem recognized as a recurring one). This view inevitably tends toward the development of patterns as elements in a generative pattern language. This is the approach taken in this book.

Support for this comes from the work of Alan O'Callaghan and his colleagues in the Object Engineering and Migration group and Software Technology Research Laboratory at De Montfort University, Leicester, UK. O'Callaghan is the lead author of the ADAPTOR pattern language for migrating legacy systems to object and component-based structures. ADAPTOR was based initially on five projects, starting in 1993, in separate business areas; it stands for Architecture-driven and Patterns-based Techniques for Object Re-engineering. It currently encapsulates experiences of eight major industrial projects in four different sectors: telecommunications, the retail industry, defence and oil exploration. O'Callaghan argues that migrating to object technology is more than mere reverse engineering, because reverse engineering is usually (a) formal and (b) focused purely on the functional nature of the legacy systems in question, and (c) assumes a self-similar architecture to the original one. The most crucial information, about the original design rationales, has already been lost irretrievably. It cannot be retrieved from the code because the code never contained that information (unless, of course, it was written in an unusually expressive way). The best that traditional archaeological approaches to reverse engineering can achieve is to recreate the old system in an object-oriented 'style' which, more often than not, delivers none of the required benefits.

The approach, suggested originally by Graham (1995) and pioneered by O'Callaghan, was to develop object models of the required 'new' system *and* the legacy systems and, by focusing on the maintainers and developers (including their organizational structure) rather than the code or design documentation, determine only subsequently what software assets might already exist that could be redeployed. O'Callaghan's group turned to patterns in the search for some way of documenting and communicating the common practices that were successful in each new project (legacy systems present especially difficult problems and are, overall, always unique unto themselves). At first, public-domain, stand-alone design patterns were used, but quickly his team were forced to mine their own. Then problems of code ownership (i.e. responsibility for part of a system being re-engineered belonging to someone other than the immediate client), caused by the fact that migrations typically involve radical changes at the level of the gross structure of a system, required that organizational and process problems be addressed also through patterns. Finally, observations that the most powerful patterns in different domains were interconnected suggested the possibility of a generative pattern language.

ADAPTOR was announced in 1998 as a 'candidate, open, generative pattern language'. It is a candidate language for two reasons: first, despite the overwhelming success of the projects from which it is drawn, ADAPTOR is not comprehensive enough in its coverage or recursed to a sufficient level of detail to be, as yet, truly generative. Secondly, O'Callaghan has different levels of confidence in the different patterns, with only those having gone through the patterns workshops of the patterns movement being regarded as fully mature. Patterns yet to prove themselves in this way are regarded as candidate patterns. ADAPTOR is open in a number of senses too. First, like any true language, both the language itself and the elements that comprise it are evolvable. Many of the most mature patterns, such as **GET THE MODEL FROM THE PEOPLE**, which was first presented in 1996 at a TelePlop workshop, have gone through numbers of iterations of change. Secondly, following Alexander *et al.* (1977), O'Callaghan insists that patterns are open abstractions themselves. Since no true pattern provides a complete solution, and every time it is applied it delivers different results (because of different specific contexts in which it is applied), it resists the kind of formalization that closed abstractions such as rules can be subject to. Finally ADAPTOR is open because it makes explicit use of other public-domain pattern languages and catalogues, such as Coplien's generative development-process language already cited, or the GoF and PoV catalogues. The *wu* language presented in Chapter 3 is also a candidate, open, generative language.

Patterns in ADAPTOR include the following:

- ◆ **GET THE MODEL FROM THE PEOPLE** requires utilization of the maintainers of a legacy system as sources of business information.

- ◆ **PAY ATTENTION TO THE FOLKLORE** treats the development/ maintenance communities as domain experts, even if they don't do so themselves.

- ◆ **BUFFER THE SYSTEM WITH SCENARIOS** gets the main business analysts, marketers, futurologists, etc. to role-play alternative business contexts to the one they bet on in their requirements specifications.

- ◆ **SHAMROCK** divides a system under development into three loosely coupled 'leaves' – each of which could contain many class categories or packages; the leaves are the conceptual domain (the problem space objects), the infrastructure domain (persistence, concurrency, etc.) and the interaction domain (GUIs, intersystem protocols, etc.).

- ◆ **TIME-ORDERED COUPLING** clusters classes according to common change rates to accommodate flexibility to change.

- ◆ **KEEPER OF THE FLAME** sets up a role whereby the detailed design decisions can be assured to be in continuity with the architecture – changes to the gross structure are permitted if deemed necessary and appropriate.

- ◆ **ARCHETYPE** creates object types to represent the key abstractions discovered in the problem space.

- ◆ **SEMANTIC WRAPPER** creates wrappers for legacy code that present behavioral interfaces of identifiable abstractions to the rest of the system.

Something of the open and generative character aspired to by ADAPTOR can be gained from looking at the typical application of patterns to the early phases of a legacy system migration project. Underpinning ADAPTOR is the model-driven approach described earlier. O'Callaghan's problem space models comprise object types and the relationships between them, which capture the behavior of key abstractions of the context of the system as well as the system itself. **ARCHETYPE** is therefore one of the first patterns used, along with **GET THE MODEL FROM THE PEOPLE** and **PAY ATTENTION TO THE FOLKLORE**. At an early stage strategic 'what-if' scenarios are run against this model using **BUFFER THE SYSTEM WITH SCENARIOS**. **SHAMROCK** is applied in order to decouple the concept domain object types from the purely system resources needed to deliver them at run time. The concept domain 'leaf' can then be factored into packages using **TIME-ORDERED COUPLING** to keep types with similar change rates (discovered through the scenario-buffering) together. Coplien's **CONWAY'S LAW** is now utilized to design a development organization that is aligned with the evolving structure of the system. **CODE OWNERSHIP** (another Coplien pattern) makes sure that every package has someone assigned to it with responsibility for it. An ADAPTOR pattern called **TRACKABLE COMPONENT** ensures that these 'code owners' are responsible for publishing the interfaces of their packages that others need to develop to, so that they can evolve in a controlled way. The GoF pattern **FAÇADE** is deployed to create scaffolding for the detailed structure of the system. It is at this point that decisions can be made as to which pieces of functionality require new code and which can make use of legacy code. The scaffolding ensures that these decisions, and their implementation consequences, can be dealt with at a rate completely under the control and at the discretion of the development team without fear of runaway ripple effects. For the latter, **SEMANTIC WRAPPERS** are used to interface the old legacy stuff to the new object-oriented bits.

Even with this cursory example we can see how the language addresses all of the important issues of architecture (client's needs, conceptual integrity, structure, process and organization, etc.) as well as getting quickly to the heart of the issues of legacy migration. O'Callaghan reports that when outlining this approach at a public tutorial, one member of the audience objected that the model-driven approach was not re-engineering at all but just 'forward engineering with the reuse of some legacy code'. In reply, O'Callaghan agreed and stated that that was just the point. On further consideration, he decided that many of ADAPTOR's patterns were not specific to legacy migration at all. As a result ADAPTOR is currently being regarded as a subset of a more general language on architectural praxis for software development in a project code-named the Janus project (O'Callaghan, 2000).

1.4   Other pattern types

Maiden *et al.* (1998) proposed a pattern language for socio-technical system design to inform requirements validation thereof, based on the CREWS-SAVRE prototype. They specify three patterns as follows:

- ◆ **MACHINE-FUNCTION:** this represents a rule connecting the presence of a user action (a task script in our language) to a system requirement to support that action (an operation of a business object that implements the task). We feel that it is stretching language somewhat to call this rule a pattern.

- ◆ **COLLECT-FIRST-OBJECTIVE-LAST:** this pattern tells us to force the user to complete the prime transaction after the subsidiary ones, e.g. ATMs should make you take the card before the cash. (For a discussion of the psychological phenomenon of completion in user interface design, see Chapter 2.)

- ◆ **INSECURE-SECURE-TRANSACTION:** this suggests that systems should monitor their security state and take appropriate action if the system becomes insecure.

The value of these patterns may be doubted because, like Fowler's analysis patterns, they seem to state the obvious; and they fail to address the sort of task or system usage patterns represented by our task association sets or use case refinement. Also, it could be argued that they are nothing but design principles – just as completion provides a well-known design principle in human–computer inter-action (HCI). On the other hand, their operationalization in the CREWS-SAVRE system indicates that they may have a specialized practical value in this and certain other contexts.

Several groups and individuals have produced patterns and pattern languages for user interface design and HCI. We will look at these in Chapter 2.

1.5   Patterns or pattern languages?

The debate about the nature of software patterns ('parameterized collaborations' versus 'design decisions', pattern catalog versus pattern languages) itself both reflects and affects debates about software architecture. That relationship has been sharply exposed by Coplien's guest editorship of *IEEE Software* magazine in the autumn of 1999. The issue was a special feature on software architecture in which Coplien published, amongst others, Alexander's keynote talk to the OOPSLA conference in San Jose, California in 1996 (Alexander, 1999). In his editorial, re-evaluating the architectural metaphor, Coplien identified two fundamental approaches to software development: the 'blueprint' or 'master plan' approach versus that of 'piecemeal growth' (Coplien, 1999). Coplien suggests that the immature discipline of software architecture is suffering from 'formal envy' and has borrowed inappropriate lessons from the worlds of both hardware engineering and the built environment. Symptoms of its crisis are the separation of the deliverables of architecture from the artefacts delivered to the customer and the reification of architecture as a separate process in a waterfall approach to software development. Following the architect of the built environment Ludwig Miles van der Rohe, Coplien proclaims, as does Alexander as we have seen, that 'God lives in the details' and that clarity at the macro level can only be judged by whether it incorporates the fine details successfully. He further asserts: 'The object experience highlights what had been important all along: architecture is not so much about software, but about the people who write the software ...' (p. 41).

The main point about coupling and cohesion is that it permits people to work socially to produce a piece of software and both recognize and value their own particular contribution. Coplien points to CRC cards and their use in object-oriented development as the classic example of software design's anthropomorphic nature. From this perspective, software patterns were the next wave in the advance of a software architectural practice of this kind. As Coplien quite rightly points out, the patterns movement has always celebrated the otherwise lowly programmer as the major source of architectural knowledge in software development. Beyond that, it recognizes the deep character of the relationship between code's structure and the communication pathways between the people developing and maintaining it. In doing so, Coplien argues, patterns have taken software development beyond the naive practice of the early days of objects, which fell short of its promise because it was still constrained by a purely modular view of software programs, inherited from the previous culture. Further advance requires liberation from the weight of 'the historic illusions of formalism and planning' (p. 42).

Richard Gabriel, who is currently a member of the Hillside Group, a master software practitioner as well as a practising poet,[4] suggests that there are two reasons why all successful software development is in reality piecemeal growth. First, there is the cognitive complexity of dealing not only with current but also possible future causes of change, which make it impossible to visualize a constructible software program in advance to the necessary level of detail with any accuracy (Gabriel, 1996). Second, there is the fact that pre-planning alienates all but the planners. Coplien, Gabriel and the entire patterns movement are dedicated to developing practices that combat this social alienation. In doing so they impart a profound social and moral obligation to the notion of software architecture. In the face of these stark realities the only alternative to piecemeal growth is the one once offered by David Parnas: fake the blueprints by reverse engineering them once the code is complete.

---

[4] The rules of the pattern writers' workshops, which are the way of working of the PLoP conferences, are attributed to Gabriel.

2 Designing user interfaces

I have heard of a man who had a mind to sell his house, and therefore carried a piece of brick in his pocket, which he shewed as a pattern to encourage purchasers.
Jonathan Swift, *The Drapier's Letters*

It is clear that the vast majority of websites are effectively unusable and the first dot coms have already bitten the dust, perhaps as a result. *Computer Weekly* (2002.01.10) reports that one-third of British sites have no search facility and 25% don't give any explanation of what their company does. Over half provide inadequate corporate data. Most of the top 100 sites were poorly rated in terms of navigation and performance. It is difficult to believe that the situation is better in other lands.

The same journal (2001.08.02) reported on the UK's Inland Revenue and their outsourcer EDS's attempts to persuade the public to submit their tax returns online. Only 39 284 people out of the 128 603 who registered managed the trick. That's a 'success' rate of less than 31%. One hapless user is quoted as saying: 'Round and round I went, but I could not find a way to get the web to accept my return. Time and time again I came back to the same screen.'

If that sounds familiar you share the experience with millions of web users. If not, you are either incredibly patient or you are a web developer: of course you can navigate around your own site.

The effect of usability on commercial success can be phenomenal. Abbey National is a British mortgage lender that reorganized its site with usability in mind in 2002. The results were a 10% increase in mortgage applications and a staggering 98% increase in the use of online calculators. Repeat visitors went up 19% and 25% more pages were visited per user. Even if there were special features in this case, it is clear that not paying attention to usability can cost a company dearly.

There are four aspects of website design: usability, content, navigation and aesthetics. The last three all contribute in some way to the first. This book offers a set of simple guidelines on how to make websites more usable. It does not cover content management or graphic design, although these important topics need to be understood too. However, it does provide a handy checklist of points to consider during site design. The checklists are constructed using a pattern language, which is set out in Chapter 3.

Many software developers will be familiar with Alexander's work on pattern languages discussed in Chapter 1. Alexander suggests that great buildings arise when egoless designers let them emerge from a pattern language, in the same way that great poetry flows from the patterns in the grammar of a spoken tongue.

There is already a substantial body of knowledge about user interface design, largely founded in cognitive psychology and anthropology. There are several published usability patterns and even an entire pattern language due to MIT's Jennifer Tidwell (www.mit.edu/~jtidwell/common_ground_onefile.html). Yet in spite of this, web designers seem to ignore this body of knowledge completely. Could the solution be a pattern language for designing usable websites?

This chapter briefly summarizes what is known about human–computer interaction (HCI) and graphical user interface (GUI) design. Chapter 3 then brings these ideas together and contains a pattern language that should make applying HCI principles to web design relatively easy.

2.1

Introduction to HCI and GUI design

**The history of
the user interface**

User interfaces originated with the very first computers in the form of cathode ray tube displays showing base 32 arithmetic for output and plug boards for input. Programming was thus like rewiring the hardware and interpreting the magic symbols that came out. The early machines also made a noise so that experienced operators could guess what sort of thing they were doing and detect abnormalities such as endless loops (a constant whirring sound). Later, Hollerith punched cards were used for input and batch line printers for output. This represented a significant advance in user friendliness – until you dropped a large box of punched cards. The main problem with this approach occurred when the programmer missed a semicolon from a line of code and discovered that the program would not compile – only after a day or so – because of this simple slip. Paper tape was not so subject to being dropped but it tore easily. Long turn-around times began to be addressed when conversational remote job entry (CRJE) was introduced, whereby the programmer could submit jobs via a golf-ball teletype machine attached to a remote computer via a modem. As television technology became cheaper to manufacture, these terminals were gradually replaced with screen terminals, which emulated CRJE devices, but quietly. For this reason, these character display terminals were known as 'glass teletypes'. In the 1970s these displays began to be used by users who were not programmers, and command line interfaces gave way to simple menu systems and tab-and-fill data entry screens. Meanwhile, Doug Englebart had invented the mouse but no one had yet exploited its potential.

The first well-known commercial application of the mouse came out of the work at Xerox PARC on the Star interface and later emerged in the form of the Apple Lisa and Macintosh. Rodents[1] made it possible to conceive of an entirely different style

---

[1] We had to call them that because foot-operated mice that run along the floor had been developed and these and the large mice used for specialist graphics work were sometimes known as **rats**.

of user interaction with the display based on the metaphor of pointing and choosing rather than instructing and describing actions. The Xerox/Apple style was emulated by many others and eventually standardized into the systems we are now familiar with, such as MS Windows and X-Windows. There have been attempts to go beyond a Windows-style interface, some based on virtual reality techniques, but little consensus on the next standard is yet evident.

Why GUI?   GUIs became popular because they are easy to use, enhance user and developer productivity, and lead to a greater degree of comfort and less stress (at least so it was widely believed). A GUI in and of itself is not the secret of productivity; it is a well-crafted GUI that is required. Interface usage also depends on the type of task being undertaken, as we shall see later. Even greater benefits derive from the consistency of the interface. In Windows, for example, no matter what application is running, the File menu is always at the top left-hand corner of the screen and Help is always the right-most pull-down menu. Even if you have no mouse, in MS Windows, Alt-F-X *always* closes the application. The exploratory style means that users can explore the structure of the application without commitment to actions. This is often achieved by 'greying out' inapplicable menu entries in the current mode, e.g. you cannot cut unless you have selected something, but you can see that cut and paste is supported in the system. An undo facility also promotes exploration since it is possible to try an action and then recover from it if the effects are undesirable. A further benefit is the use of a metaphor, the so-called desktop metaphor, to help users transfer knowledge from manual tasks to using the computer. We will discuss such transfer effects in more detail later.

The uses to which GUIs can be put are manifold. They can be used to hide multi-language implementations, systems connected by loosely coupling systems written in different products. A very common use of GUIs is to protect users from the interaction style of old mainframe systems or the complexities of networks. All these usages can be viewed as examples of object wrappers, when the GUI is built using an object-oriented language.

The apparent, main benefits of GUIs are consistency, ease of use, learnability and the ease with which multiple applications can be combined. However, there are drawbacks, including extra software, hardware, operational and support costs, and more complex software development. The rapid expansion of standard memory and hard disk capacity during the 1990s is mainly a tribute to the hardware hunger of GUIs. On the other hand, the cash price of such a machine did not change appreciably. Even had this not been the case, these extra costs would have been paid for by better, more usable, more flexible applications and the consequent business benefits.

Designing the HCI   Design for HCI is like other design problems and the same principles apply. Designed artefacts should be fit for their purpose. They should be natural in behavior and conform to users' expectations. There should be no unpleasant surprises except where these are introduced deliberately as alarms. Use of the artefact should give feedback on progress of the task being undertaken. They should fit the mental and manual abilities of users. A very common example of bad interface design outside the context of computers concerns door handles. Some time ago, the present author was walking through an office building with a colleague and, meeting a closed door, he grasped its handle and pushed. Nothing happened because the door only opened toward him. His colleague laughed and remarked that his old headmaster would have shouted: 'Stupid boy! Can't you see that the handle is there to be pulled?' He had to explain that he had worked for over two years in a building that had handles on both sides of all the doors and that he had often strained himself by pulling doors that should be pushed. In the end he had become totally disoriented in his relationships with all doors. Don Norman (1988) documented the same phenomenon. The stupidity of builders or architects that design in this way is still quite exasperating. Further, someone pays them for the work: more stupid yet! We know of at least two systems that include the helpful advice: Press Enter to Exit. And, as we have to explain patiently to Mac users, to close down Windows you click on Start; obviously! As long as users continue to buy them, designers will continue to deliver such daft interfaces.

Similar examples of inane design abound. Our feeling is that a good design is one that supports a conversational style of interaction. Barfield (1993) compares a computer with a human servant and pillories bad interface designers by asking how we would respond if such a servant replied to simple requests with sentences like 'Error code 42 Sir!' Worse, he argues, if it behaves like the servant who, when asked to put a fiction writer's new manuscript in the filing cabinet, returns with the comment: 'Sorry Sir, the filing cabinet was full so I burnt the manuscript.'

Criticizing other people's design is far easier than designing something well yourself. This chapter attempts to set out a series of guidelines for good user interface design, including good practice in the analysis required to design well. A key technique is task analysis, which is used widely by successful designers (pattern 3). The key observation here is that user-centred design and, especially, the task-centerd design favoured by most user interface theorists are important for creating usable, useful, correct systems – even where the interface element is not the primary consideration. First, we pause to look at some hardware issues.

Selecting the hardware

Hardware for the user interface may be conveniently divided into hardware for input, output or both. There are many kinds of input device available, including plug boards, punched cards, paper tape, keyboards (QWERTY and otherwise), mice, tracker balls, light pens, pressure pens, joysticks, data gloves, graphics tablets, touch screens and microphones. There are several types of touch screen, including scanning infra-red, surface acoustic wave, capacitative overlay and conductive or resistive membrane types. This is not the place to discuss these in detail but continuous capacitative touch screens are probably agreed to be best for most kinds of application. In the common imagination, voice input must be the ideal form of input for the majority of tasks. There is no learning time because we mostly know a natural language already. It leaves our hands and eyes free and imposes a very low cognitive load due to the commonplace character of speech. On the other hand, there are many disadvantages. Speech can be noisy and distracting to others in the work environment, and voice input itself needs silence since ambient noise can interfere with the interpretation. Complex software is needed and in practice there is a trade-off between the training time required and a limited vocabulary. Correct interpretation can be affected by illness, alcohol, the weather, and so on.

Though voice input is attractive for many applications, especially those where the user's hands are not free, there are problems with the recognition of continuous speech. To see why this is so consider the sentence: 'It's very hard to wreck a nice beach'. Now try saying it out loud a few times, rapidly.[2] There are now continuous speech recognition systems but their vocabulary is very limited. The topic remains essentially in the research domain. Most speech input systems make fairly precise impositions on what can be said and how, or require time-consuming training to recognize one user's voice patterns. There are several products allowing authors to speak text into their word processors, providing that they are prepared to spend a quite considerable time training the system.

As well as devices for input, there are several options for the output devices, including screens, printers and loudspeakers. Networks are both input and output devices. Only input devices, such as screens, raise serious HCI issues, not mostly concerned with physical ergonomics. However, voice – and indeed musical – output has become very important on the web, one example being the provision of web services to the blind (pattern 51).

Virtual reality, which immerses the user in a simulated world and provides feedback through multiple senses as well as multiple media, offers perhaps the greatest challenge of all to user interface designers. Fortunately, all interactions in such a world can be described as interactions with objects satisfying contracts. However, it is not yet clear what the new psychological factors associated with immersion are. Many of the basic user interface principles may need amendment and much care is needed since there are many medical and social dangers.

Studies have shown that there is no 'best' input or output device. What is most appropriate and usable depends not only on

---

[2] If there was someone within earshot while you were doing this, they are probably agreeing with you by now that is indeed very hard to recognize speech.

the application but also on the precise task or set of tasks being carried out. One unpublished study, carried out by Logica, concluded that foreign exchange traders would benefit from a keyboard but that a bond trader might do better using a graphics tablet for input. Given changes in both the task and the technology, whether these results apply today is unclear.

Of course, the web offers little choice of hardware to most of its users. The vast majority have a small screen, a keyboard and a mouse. A growing number have the facilities to interact via a microphone or a web-camera but it would be a mistake to design a public site that relied on such devices, except for specialist applications aimed at particular communities. Pattern 10 deals with this limitation.

2.2   Designing interaction

Styles of interaction

There are many different ways of interacting with a computer system. These include menus, forms, command languages, natural language and GUIs. As with input and output devices, the best style of interaction depends mainly on the task being undertaken. There is no generic best style.

Menus have the advantage that they can be learnt quickly. They generally require fewer keystrokes than other styles and can use dialog management tools. Menus help to give structure to the dialog and make it far easier for the designer to manage errors. However, there are several disadvantages too. The menu tree may be deep and difficult to remember and navigate. This may slow down frequent users significantly. Menus consume screen space, are inflexible and impose a need for a rapid display rate. The most significant factor with menu interfaces is the need for the task analysis to be complete.

Forms-based interfaces are mainly suitable for data entry and tend to make it easier. Users of such interfaces require modest training but they are not very good for casual users – which most web users are. They too consume screen space and tend to be inflexible.

Modal dialog boxes, where the dialog is constrained strictly to the questions and values in the current box, represent a sort of combination of the forms- and menus-based approaches.

Command languages have the advantage of infinite flexibility and are usually tailorable with macros or a programming language. However, they are notoriously hard to learn, hard to remember and easy to make errors with.

The oldest command languages are natural languages and it has often been remarked that the computer should speak the user's language and interact in English or some other natural language. This would mean that the users had no new commands to learn but there are several very serious disadvantages. Natural languages are expressive but verbose and ambiguous. In work situations, even without computers, a more formal or structured subset of language is often used. Consider, for example, the use of 'roger' in military communications or technical jargon in most trades. Natural language conversations are invariably based on implicit, shared understanding and the fact that when this breaks down clarification is often needed – and this will slow dialogs unbearably. This and the context sensitivity of language mean that artificial intelligence techniques are required. Unfortunately, these techniques are not very advanced yet and some of us believe that a speaking computer would be a thinking computer and that that is either impossible or so far beyond the scope of rational human engineering as to be absurd (Graham, 1994). Natural language front-ends to databases have been written and exist as commercial products, but these do not attempt to solve the general language understanding problem, preferring rather to permit natural enquiries in a restricted context, based on a shared model of the data dictionary and its structure.

Fundamentals of cognitive psychology

In order to design a good user interface, it is necessary to know a little about the way the human mind and body work. In particular it is useful to know how memory storage and retrieval works, how the eye responds to colors, what positions lead to fatigue, and so on. The bodily aspects of human–computer interaction are often referred to as ergonomics, though strictly this subject encompasses the mental aspects as well.

Pattern 18 discusses those aspects of cognitive psychology that site designers need to be aware of. These include the concepts of long-term memory (LTM) and working (or activated) memory (WM) and the way they are related. It also discusses the related phenomena of rehearsal, priming, transfer effects and interference.

There are several guidelines that can be deduced from a knowledge of how users act when reading displays. Research has shown that the first items read from a list tend to be stored more readily in LTM. This is known as the **primacy effect**. The last items in a list tend to be stored in WM: the **recency effect**. One corollary of this is the need for interfaces to be standardized across applications and stable in time. Standard interfaces also exploit the classification structures of memory.

Standard user interfaces are important because of the memory limitations of users. The chief advantage of any GUI is that most applications work in the same way and we can utilize positive transfer when closing a window or calling for help because the positions of the features are standard. In our opinion, this is more important than ease of use itself. Pattern 36 emphasizes this.

Another important principle of user interface design that derives from an understanding of psychology is exploiting closure, which is covered by Pattern 39.

Cognitive dissonance occurs when a false consciousness is created to explain a bad design. Users create explanations for doing stupid things. If you do something often enough and have worked hard to learn how to do it, you will often invent reasons for continuing to do so. In this way, bad designs become right by usage and bugs become features. Having invested the learning time, you can make yourself an indispensable resource as the source of knowledge about the product. Now you can be the expert to whom others refer, even though a better-designed product would eliminate the need for any expertise. We have observed this often with impenetrable mainframe operating systems, otiose programming languages such as RPG, and write-only macro languages such as that of Lotus 123 and its ilk. Perhaps the QWERTY keyboard could be regarded as a particularly well-known example of this phenomenon.

Given this very high level knowledge of psychological principles, we can now establish some practical principles and guidelines for HCI design.

**Principles
for HCI design**

HCI involves computers, users, tasks and requirements. For a time, user-centerd design was emphasized. However, it is now widely realized that the user is not a stable given, because users adopt varying roles in interacting with a computer system. The stable feature is often the task being performed for the role. Therefore, this section and this whole book focus on task-centerd design. HCI uses principles from computer science, psychology, sociology, anthropology, engineering, aesthetics and many other areas. This book emphasizes insights from psychology, software engineering and knowledge engineering but attempts to take account of all other influences. The main insight from knowledge engineering is that the user interface includes the user's knowledge of the system and the system's model of the user.

It is crucial that the interface designer, like the software engineer, does not stop at analyzing and automating existing manual practices. Computers can change the tasks they were designed to assist with, and this is often their largest contribution. Word processing has largely changed the nature of work in many offices and the impact of the web continues the trend.

HCI design involves the following issues:

◆ Functionality: how does the interface help users carry out tasks and how does it impede them? Does the interface itself make something possible or impossible?

◆ Aesthetics.

◆ Acceptability.

◆ Structure.

◆ Reliability.

◆ Efficiency.

◆ Maintainability.

◆ Extensibility.

- Cost.

- Usability, covering, learnability, memorability, productivity, propensity to make errors, support for tasks (task analysis), safety and range of users.

- Suitability for different locations and conditions.

Prototyping is widely seen as essential for the production of usable interfaces. Some authorities recommend the use of specialist graphic or industrial designers as part of the development team and some go further, suggesting the complete separation of the user interface development within the lifecycle. We think that this is a mistake and that sound practices of software engineering should integrate the specialist skills of interface designers into those of software developers in general. There is a danger here that these remarks will be interpreted to mean that developers can just design the interface from the use cases; which is in fact what the Rational Unified Process (RUP) recommends. Of course, the use cases do *define* the permissible interactions, but we must also *design* each interaction. To do this requires the developer to become an expert user interface designer. Because GUIs are so important, we believe that most developers should acquire such skills as the norm; if you can't then you'll have to hire a specialist. Alan Cooper (1999) concurs with this view in contrast to most of the HCI community, such as Jakob Nielsen, who usually recommend hiring specialists rather than changing the orientation of developers.

It is remarkable that the most liked features of a given GUI are often the aesthetic ones. One of the most popular innovations in windows systems, for example, was the 3D push button that appears to depress when clicked or held clicked. It apparently contributes nothing, but it is loved by users to the extent of being a prerequisite for all such systems nowadays.

General HCI principles are rare, although some have been suggested. IBM's (1992) CUA (Common User Access) gave a set of remarkably clear and complete guidelines that are compatible with an object-oriented approach. It incorporated task analysis, user surveys, site visits and usability testing within the approach and constructs three models representing user, designer and programmer views on the interface and underlying system. CUA emphasized reducing user memory load, consistency and placing the user in command of the interface. In particular, in support of the last principle, it recommends not blaming users for errors, parsimonious use of modes with pre-emption to control them, immediate feedback, undo, accommodating users with different skill levels, providing helpful messages, customizability and transparency of the interface. Using meaningful class interfaces to control interaction and using concrete instances and examples wherever possible reduces memory loads. The CUA approach to consistency exploits the principles of aesthetics, continuity and priming via clear standards and visual metaphors. Object-oriented processes such as Feature Driven Design (FDD), RUP and Perspective are deficient in this area (Coad *et al.*, 1999: Kruchten, 1999; Allen and Frost, 1998).

Generic principles   Thimbleby (1990) introduced the concept of Generative User-Engineering Principles (GUEPs) for both designers and users. Typical GUEPs he identifies include the following:

◆ Recognize and exploit closure (Pattern 39).

◆ WYSIWYG = What You See Is What You Get! (Cf Pattern 70).

◆ Fix the documentation and then make the program conform to it.

◆ The designer should be able to explain the interface concisely and completely.

◆ The designer must ensure that the user can construct an appropriate internal, mental model of the system.

He also introduces a number of formal or algebraic GUEPs as follows:

◆ *Idempotence* $[T = T^2]$ (Pattern 22).

◆ *Distributivity* $[A*(B+C) = A*B+A*C]$. This principle says that distributing operations over their arguments can enhance usability and convenience by reducing input. For example, 'delete file1; delete file2' should be equivalent to 'delete file1, file2'. In MS Windows Explorer, *delete file* distributes over *select file*, so that you can select a whole bunch of files and delete them at one stroke.

◆ *Commutativity* [A*B = B*A]. This says that the order of operations should not be important unless order is significant. For example, cursor movement (except at the screen boundaries) with the right and left arrow keys successively should leave the cursor position unchanged. This principle tends against the common modern innovation of permitting mouse wrap-around where the mouse appears on the opposite side of the screen when moved past the boundary (Pattern 22).

◆ *Substitutivity* means putting an expression in place of a constant, as can be done in most programming languages or spreadsheets.

◆ *Associativity* [A*(B*C) = (A*B)*C]. This principle is equivalent to that of modelessness (Pattern 40).

◆ *Equal opportunity.* Output can become input and vice versa (e.g. aperture or shutter priority cameras) (Pattern 65).

Other design principles that we advocate are the following.

◆ **WYSIWYG.** This term has been mentioned already without explaining it. It stands for What You See Is What You Get (*cf* Pattern 70).

◆ **WYSIWYCU** stands for What You See Is What You Can Use (Pattern 70).

◆ The principle of **commensurate effort** states that it should be as hard to delete something as to create it; as hard to undo as to do. Steve Jobs' slogan 'Simple things should be simple, difficult things should be possible' is a rephrasing of this principle.

◆ The interface should provide a **sense of progress** (Pattern 48).

◆ **Non-pre-emption** (Pattern 66).

◆ **Self-demonstrability.** Consider context-sensitive help, tutorials and – best of all – a completely intuitive interface based on transfer effects from a suitable metaphor.

◆ **Options should be settable by the user.** For example, the Microsoft Mouse driver offers options for wrapping the pointer round to the opposite screen edge and snapping its position to the latest OK button to appear in a dialog box. Both these options are useful but to the experienced user just lead to 'mouse creep' as the physical position is constantly at variance with his expectations. Fortunately, they can be switched off. It is often quite difficult to do this on the web.

◆ **Avoid frequent channel switching.** Frequent switching of input between keyboard and mouse is evidently undesirable. Distracting messages from screen areas other than the one where attention is directed should be avoided, as should moving the focus of attention around too much.

So much for principles; now for some practical advice on user interface design.

Guidelines for user interface design

In the context of a user interface, both the user and the system must fulfil their responsibilities towards each other based on the known use cases. The responsibilities of the user include knowing what tasks can be attempted, being able to perform the procedures needed to accomplish these tasks, understanding and interpreting messages (including their interpretation under different modes) and being able to use the appropriate input/output devices. The responsibilities of the system include helping the user to carry out the tasks specified during design, responding correctly to commands, pre-empting destructive input, meeting performance constraints and sometimes explaining itself to the user. These responsibilities are task oriented rather than user oriented because the same user may have quite different responsibilities when adopting a different role when a different set of tasks is implied. For example, the same user might approach the systems as a manager enquiring on performance or as a data-entry clerk adding new financial assumptions.

Designers should remember that there are considerable variations among users. Icons – images – are culturally dependent as demonstrated by the icon in **WORDS BEFORE ICONS** (57). Furthermore, users vary widely in their visual ability and will react accordingly. In addition to this natural variation in ability there may also be very great variation due to handicaps such as color blindness, missing fingers, fatigue, illiteracy, memory disorders, deafness, and so on.

The **power law of practice** says that practice has a log-linear effect on skill or that practice makes perfect. The more opportunity the users have to explore the interface, the better they will become at using it. This implies that both regular use and an exploratory style will help. It also tells us that systems that will be used by infrequent users need more attention to the user interface.

Users come to the system with different backgrounds and knowledge levels. Psychology tells us that during skill acquisition, knowledge is first stored as **declarative knowledge**, often in the form of rules and objects to which those rules apply, and can be directly recalled as such. Practice helps people store associations between items and form chunks based on these associations; this is **associative knowledge**. More practice compiles the rules into **procedural knowledge** by which stage it is often inaccessible to consciousness, as with the knowledge of how to ride a bicycle or read a sentence. On this basis, designers should design for the knowledge level of the users they anticipate using the systems and preferably provide both novice and expert modes.

Here are some commonly used heuristics for user interface modeling which add to the above principles:

◆ Use strong, natural metaphors and analogies.

◆ Keep it simple (Pattern 38).

◆ Model the domain objects directly (Pattern 3).

◆ Use semantic structures (classification, composition, usage, association).

◆ Minimize semantic primitives.

◆ Capture rules (Pattern 3).

◆ Remember that documentation, training and the user's knowledge are all part of the user interface.

Dialog design

Dialog design is a problem for all user interfaces, graphical or otherwise. Much work outside computer science may be drawn upon. Relevant fields include discourse analysis and semiotics. Speech act theory (Austin, 1962; Searle, 1969) is particularly relevant to groupware systems (Winograd and Flores, 1986) and has influenced our approach to requirements modeling (Graham, 2001; Patterns 1–3). Suchman (1987) applies anthropological and ethnomethodological principles to the design of photocopiers. Johnson (1992) describes a number of research attempts to formalize interaction using command language grammars and task action languages. Neither approach is yet proven to yield significant improvements in practice. Perhaps the most important observation that can be made in this context is that dialogs depend on shared understanding and knowledge of a common domain. This has long been known to designers of computerized natural language systems where it would be a wonderful achievement to get a computer to understand the sentence 'time flies like an arrow' because of the use of simile but how much harder it is to expect the same machine to respond intelligently, and soon after the last remark, to the observation that 'fruit flies like a banana'.

Dialogs are used for several reasons: to give commands, to refine a common goal and plan tasks to achieve it, to convey information, data or knowledge, to pass the time. Most system dialogs are concerned with commands and conveying information and data. Commands imply a commitment on the part of the recipient to carry out the task mentioned. All interactions initiated by the user should therefore give an observable result, either confirming that the task is complete and giving any resultant information or reporting an exception. This goes beyond the goal of the use case. In other words, well-designed systems are *helpful*. They should also be *forgiving* of user errors.

Expert systems often include explanation facilities, although the latter are more costly to write than is often supposed. Sometimes, therefore, a dialog consists of an explanation that modifies the user's model of the system. If the user has a good model of a system, they will find it easier to use. Good feedback as well as explanation helps the user to develop and refine a model. If the system has a model of the user, it will be able to respond more appropriately. Examples of the latter occur frequently in intelligent computer-aided learning, where the system asks easier questions of novices based on their test scores, or in systems that have a *novice* and *expert* mode switch of some sort.

Here are some heuristics for dialog design:

◆ Minimize input movements.

◆ Maximize input bandwidth/channels.

◆ The interface should look good (Pattern 16).

◆ Be consistent (keys, positioning, etc.) (Patterns 24 and 26).

◆ Follow standards (Pattern 36).

◆ Ease of use should be paramount (Pattern 38).

◆ Keep the system modeless or provide a high level of context-sensitive feedback (Pattern 40).

◆ A natural response time is desirable (Pattern 42).

◆ Use words and language carefully (Pattern 50).

◆ Make it non-pre-emptive (Pattern 66).

◆ Process continuity should be sought (Pattern 75).

◆ Make your system customizable.

Usability tests and metrics

Evaluation of the user interface is very important. HCI reviews and expert walkthroughs are usually enormously useful. Other valuable evaluation techniques include questionnaires, observational studies and test script reports. Useful GUI metrics include the time it takes to learn an operation or to use a whole system, the time it takes to carry out a particular task, the average user's error rate, satisfaction indices and the skill retention over time. These metrics imply that a budget for experimentation and data collection should be created. Also, it should be noted that the existing system should be measured with respect to these metrics during requirements capture if the metrics are to be of use in assessing benefits.

For mass-market products, it is often worth investing in full-scale usability workshops wherein trial users are recorded, observed and measured carrying out common operations. This is usually too expensive for custom developments, but it would be worthwhile for systems going into very wide use or where paybacks are very high and sensitive to usability. Observational studies of any kind imply the need for usability metrics to be agreed. One can measure learnability by comparing task execution times before and after extended use. Usability testing is easier if it is supported by specific software support tools, although this is most beneficial for mature products where comparisons with earlier versions are possible. Usability testing also uses task analysis as a key technique.

Usability tests should examine users' roles, skill levels, frequency of use and the possible social, cultural and organizational variations. Use case analysis emphasizes the centrality of user roles; that is, neither the users nor their roles but the combination of a user adopting a role: an actor. This notion combines the skill level and organizational role in a single, finer-grained concept. Usability studies may further distinguish computer and application skill levels and most approaches to HCI use a simple knowledge-level model such as:

1 Beginner (no knowledge).

2 Learner (knowledge incomplete, encoded as rules).

3 Competent (knowledge complete, compiled and not accessible to consciousness).

4 Expert (knowledge subject to critique and refinement).

Usability testing requires careful experimental design and statistical analysis. It is therefore expensive. At the simplest level it must identify the categories of the most frequent users, such as, frequent, competent with computers, domain learners, English-speaking or well-educated. The tests should take account of transfer effects between different environments and this may, for example, lead to the need for a user interface that looks the same on different platforms. An additional difficulty with testing GUIs arises from their graphical nature. Whereas a command line interface can be tested by producing a test harness that compares textual output across trials, often GUI tests have to compare bitmaps of output. This is complicated by the need to ignore irrelevant variations, such as the final position of the mouse pointer, which makes careful design of the tests very important. For all this, big savings can result from thorough usability engineering.

The next chapter contains a group of patterns concerning testing (Patterns 6–9), but the details of how to go about usability testing are outside of the scope of the *wu* pattern language.

2.3   Usability patterns

There have been several initiatives concerned with patterns for general HCI and GUI design. General information on HCI patterns can be found at www.stanford.edu/~borchers/hcipatterns/.

A group at the University of Brighton have a collection of patterns that includes the following:

1 ALLOW TYPE AHEAD

2 GIVE A WARNING

3 INTERACTION FEEDBACK

4 JUST LOOKING

5 SHOW COMPUTER IS THINKING

6 SHOW THE FORMAT REQUIRED

7 THE MVC ARCHITECTURE

8 THINK TWICE

9 TIME TO DO SOMETHING ELSE

10 BUFFERING MAY BE DANGEROUS

11 GET CONFIRMATION

12 GET AUTHORIZATION

13 AUTOMATIC OVERRIDE

14 DESKTOP METAPHOR

15 GRAPHICAL USER INTERFACE

16 ALWAYS INDICATE CURRENT MODE

17 PROMPT FOR INPUT

18 ALLOW UNDO

19 IMPLEMENT THE USER'S MENTAL MODEL

20 EMERGENCY EXITS

21 SAVE THE WORK

Some of these patterns are related, but the collection is not quite a pattern language. The names of the patterns make most of their intentions self-explanatory. The Brighton Usability Pattern Collection is no longer at http://www.it.bton.ac.uk/cil/ but the authors can be contacted via this site.

Other HCI pattern initiatives include Tom Erickson's Interaction Design Pattern Page and LinguaFranca sites. The latter discusses pattern languages for HCI (www.pliant.org/personal/Tom_ Erickson/InteractionPatterns.html, www.pliant.org/personal/Tom_ Erickson/LinguaFranca_ DIS2000.html).

These sites also contain useful links to other relevant sites.

The Amsterdam Collection of Patterns in User Interface Design contains some web usability patterns, namely:

◆ Navigation patterns: **BREADCRUMBS, DOUBLE TAB, META-NAVIGATION, OUTGOING LINKS, SPLIT NAVIGATION, REPEATED MENU.**

◆ Page elements: **NEWS BOX, LIST BUILDER, TABBING, PAGING, WIZARD, PARTS SELECTOR, LANGUAGE SELECTOR.**

◆ Searching patterns: **SIMPLE SEARCH, ADVANCED SEARCH, SEARCH AREA, SITEMAP.**

◆ E-commerce patterns: **SHOPPING CART, IDENTIFY, REGISTERING.**

Clearly, some of these patterns are identical in purpose to the ones in this book. The site is at www.cs.vu.nl/~martijn/patterns/index.html.

Todd Coram and Jim Lee give a pattern language for user interface design called Experiences: www.maplefish.com/todd/papers/ experiences/Experiences.html.

Robert Orenstein offers a pattern language for HTML 2.0: www. anamorph.com/docs/patterns/default.html.

Dave Orme gives his website patterns at http://c2.com/cgi-bin/wiki?WebsitePatterns.

One of the most complete user interface pattern languages is Common Ground from MIT's Jennifer Tidwell. Although the web is not her specific concern, many of her patterns are relevant to web design and some overlap with the patterns in this book. For example, Tidwell's **HIGH-DENSITY INFORMATION DISPLAY** maps on to our **SHORT TEXTS** and to what Tufte (1983, 1990) calls chart junk. Tidwell's **STATUS DISPLAY** is related to our **USE OF COLOR** and **MANDATORY FIELDS** patterns. Her **NAVIGABLE SPACES** generates our **SITE MAP**. Her **DISABLED IRRELEVANT THINGS** generates our **OBLIQUE LANDMARKS** and **WYSIWYCU. HIERARCHICAL SET** is expressed in the way we have organized our language. There are many other points of correspondence. Many of her patterns are either irrelevant or wrong in a web context because of the limitations of browser technology but it is well worth visiting (www.mit. edu/~jtidwell/common_ground_onefile.html).

Our presentation of the patterns in *wu* was strongly influenced by the way Borchers (2001) is organized. He describes three small pattern languages laid out very much in the style of Alexander. The first contains patterns for learning to play the blues and the other two are concerned with HCI and software development, all based on experience building an interactive music exhibit for a Viennese museum. Most of the patterns are domain specific but they are beautifully written and we are sure that musicians will love the first language. We were also influenced by the hierarchical organization of his patterns. Borchers also gives a useful précis of Tidwell's HCI language.

Despite the plethora of work on user interface patterns and even some very recent work on pattern languages for web usability, such as that of van Duyne *et al.* (2002), we think that our perspective is unique, as we shall explain in the next chapter.

2.4   Bibliographical notes

Schneiderman (1987) has been a standard text on user interface design for some time. It is particularly good on the use of specific types of hardware for input and output. Laurel (1990) discusses the art of user interface design in general and in relation to several emerging technologies. It collects several papers on the design aspects of systems using advanced user interface technology, including virtual reality. Laurel's most interesting work is concerned with applying the principles of Greek drama to interface design. Suchman (1987) applies anthropological and ethnomethodological principles to user interface design and gives, as an example, the case study design of a photocopier interface at Xerox Corporation. Suchman approaches design from the point of view that the user is acting within the context of a certain situation and that the machine should be sensitive to this situation as far as possible. Johnson (1992) deals with task analysis and especially the knowledge analysis of tasks. There are many other references on task analysis that may be usefully consulted too. Thimbleby (1990) is a thoughtful contribution to the subject and some of the abstract patterns in *wu* are derived from his work. The work of Brown and Duguid (1996) is expressed in our KISS pattern.

Norman (1988) is essential background reading for user interface designers. Design patterns are related closely to object-oriented application frameworks. Another classic is Cooper (1995).

Lee (1993) gives a reasonably complete and well-structured approach to GUI design based on object-oriented principles. The emphasis is on task analysis and interface design principles. Lee describes how to perform usability studies and bases his method of task analysis on the traditional 'goals, operators, methods and selection rules' model. He simplifies this model by expressing tasks as simple subject/predicate sentences and explains the approach well using a running personnel administration example. Especially clear guidelines on the use of user interface metaphors such as the desktop metaphor are provided and the architectural design of GUIs is covered briefly.

Baecker and Buxton (1987) provide a comprehensive collection of source papers on early user interface design theory, including many that pre-date the arrival of graphical interfaces. The proceedings of the various annual conferences on the subject of HCI will take the reader further.

The classic text on web usability is by Jakob Nielsen (2000) and Krug (2000) adds much useful advice. Nielsen and Tahir (2002) concentrate on home page design and give useful guidelines. Veen

(2001) is much more practical and is not above giving useful HTML hints and tricks. Spool *et al.* (1999) base their advice on an extensive usability survey. Cato (2001) majors on usability testing. All these texts have influenced the *wu* pattern language. Van Duyne *et al.* (2002) became available only as we were going to press but influenced some patterns.

Other books on web usability that may be of interest include those by Donnelly (2000), Guidice and Dennis (2001), Valqui and Freire (2001), Burns (2001) and Navarro (2001).

3 The *wu* pattern language

So thou wilt woo
Shakespeare, *Romeo and Juliet*, Act 2 Scene 2

This chapter describes in detail a pattern language for the design of usable websites. It is the largest and the most central chapter in this book, designed to be a handy reference for web designers as well as an exposition of the language. Because the language is concerned with web usability and because we want to emphasize that it is a language rather than a pattern catalog, it is tempting to call it *wu*, acronymically. This is serendipitous since Wu is a natural language, or perhaps rather a group of dialects, spoken in eastern China. The best known of these is Shanghaihua (Shanghainese). Wu is also a common family name and the designation for one of the historic Three Kingdoms (AD 220–265). If you ever find the need to say it out loud, beware. Pronounce it as though it were followed by a question mark, i.e. with a rising tone. Otherwise you could be saying something quite different – and possibly improper. To avoid embarrassment and ambiguity, we have used the simplified Chinese character for Wu as a graphical motif throughout this text, signifying nothing in particular. So, with no apology to those of you who couldn't care less, back to business.

3.1   Basics

Using the language   The simplest way to use the *wu* language is to consider pattern number one (**ESTABLISH THE BUSINESS OBJECTIVES**) first and then follow the links to the other patterns. It is best to have a concrete problem in mind when doing this. Eventually you will reach patterns that are terminal. You can also construct sublanguages to deal with specific design problems or specific kinds of site. This is discussed further in Chapter 4.

The language consists of a network of highly interconnected patterns. Generally speaking, these links represent the order in which one would use or consider the patterns in the design process. This book is supported by a website that represents the connections between patterns by hyperlinks. In order to simplify the language as much as possible, we have tried to stick as closely as possible to a hierarchical structure. However, to do so everywhere would take away some of the language's power.

To assist in presentation and navigation, we have divided the language into four sections representing roughly the temporal order in which one might use them. These sections are dealt with by the last four sections of this chapter and have been labelled as patterns for:

◆ getting started on your site;

◆ enhancing usability;

◆ adding detail;

◆ dealing with workflow and security.

Pattern numbering is continuous across these sections to emphasize their rather arbitrary nature. Each section starts with a map of that section of the language that provides a high-level overview of the section and – on the website – provides primary navigation. The maps, although not the sections, may overlap slightly. In these maps, the patterns are classified into abstract, concrete and terminal patterns as shown by their color coding.

Abstract, concrete and terminal patterns

Abstract patterns represent the codification of principles, often derived from subjects such as cognitive psychology or ergonomics. Unlike concrete patterns, they usually have no initial context. An example of an abstract pattern that derives more from common sense than from scientific endeavour is **KISS (38)**. This pattern encodes the principles of simplicity that Jakob Nielsen has argued for so cogently and passionately over the last few years. There can be no context for such a principle; it's just always a useful one and informs the way downstream patterns are applied and interpreted.

Concrete patterns are patterns in the usual sense and we discuss their structure in detail below.

Finally, some patterns are terminal with this language.

The scope and boundaries of the language

Patterns being terminal does not mean that design thinking stops with them – merely that the language considers the further design issues as beyond its scope or ambitions. For example, we do not consider patterns that do not concern usability specifically. Such patterns evidently exist: detailed patterns for attracting more visitors to your site or upping advertising revenue for instance. The other cases where the language terminates abruptly usually concern areas of some complexity that, in our opinion, are deserving of pattern language in their own right. The examples that spring to mind are designing sites for the physically or mentally handicapped and making the site attractive to look at – the sort of thing that you need a good graphic designer for. Clearly, both areas concern usability but we quail at including the complexities of these topics. First, it would make the language large, and large things are generally unwieldy and hard to use. Second, we do not feel especially competent in these areas. We would encourage those others who are competent to set about building languages for these important topics.

Personalization is a borderline case. It is clear that personalization influences usability but it is not clear exactly how. One can state that when personalization works, usability should be enhanced but it is possible that badly thought-out personalization could make a site less usable for some of its users. For example, we recall being irritated by Amazon's recommendations on several occasions – not a very serious defect admittedly but bad nevertheless. We decided not to include it within *wu* because we felt that not enough was known about it at this time to justify its ossification in a pattern. So, while it is an important and interesting topic it remains out of scope at present. Work on a pattern language for personalization has been started by Koch and Rossi (2002).

Another case is borderline. Veen (2001) commends the use of cascading style sheets (CSS) to help separate presentation from content, thus assisting with maintenance and usability. CSS is a standard for describing how content should appear on HTML pages by adding tags and instructions to the browser as to how these tags should be rendered. One can control things like fonts and margins very effectively in this way – though not as well as with the projected XML tags of Tim Berners-Lee's semantic web we suspect. In the end, we decided that CSS was a technique just outside of the scope of *wu*. If we had included it, we would have called it, following Veen, **GETTING STYLISH**.

Abstract patterns are never terminal of course.

References to patterns are always set in **BOLD, SANS SERIF SMALL CAPITALS**. On the *wu* website these become hyperlinks to the patterns concerned.

Patterns always start on a new page.

Rules are made to be broken. The patterns in the chapter may be regarded as rules for successful design but it is better to think of them as providing suggestions, guidance and checklists of things not to forget to think about. If you do find yourself treating the patterns as rules, then pause. Always consider the likely effects of breaking the rules and ensure that you understand the rules that you are going to break and the justification for doing so.

The structure of a pattern

Each pattern is presented using the same layout, semantic structure and typographical conventions. These are based very closely on the structure pioneered by Alexander *et al.* (1977). The **pattern number** and **name** are presented first in green followed, optionally, by a list of alternative names. The latter, if present, are labelled **AKA** (also known as) in the margin. Next comes what many people call a **sensitizing image**: a picture or diagram concerning, supporting or illustrating the pattern. In many, but by no means all, cases this is a screen shot taken from a website.

After the sensitizing image we present the **context** in which one would normally encounter the pattern. With the exception of some abstract patterns, this section usually gives the names of patterns that one has already used or considered. This is separated from the body of the pattern by three green tildes, thus:

~ ~ ~

Next, the **problem** is stated in bold blue text. For the discussion of the **forces** that are at work and the way the pattern deals with them we return to plain text, i.e. text of the sort you are reading in this paragraph. This section may include quite diverse types of commentary and explanations. Where appropriate, we highlight known uses of the patterns. Where this is omitted, it is because the known uses are so obvious as to not need stating or because they have been intrinsic to the description of the forces and related discussion.

Once the discussion is complete, we state or summarize the recommended **solution** in bold blue text. This section is highlighted in the margin with the word **Therefore**. This completes the body of the pattern, so we again delimit it with three green tildes.

The next section describes the **resultant context** and, unless the pattern is terminal, will include the names of the patterns that one may consider applying next. This information is partly represented in Figure 3.1 by dotted arrows. Interpret these arrows as meaning 'supplies a potential context for'. Using the *wu* website, one may go directly to these patterns by clicking on their names in the text.

Finally, we acknowledge contributions from people who attended Ian Graham's workshops or visited the virtual workshop on our website and commented, adding ideas. In some cases, this includes acknowledging the source literature from which we have distilled the pattern.

Star rating

Again, following Alexander, we have classified the patterns according to our degree of confidence in them. The pattern's 'star rating', shown next to its name in orange, indicates this. Three stars means that we are totally convinced of the pattern's efficacy, having used it or seen it used successfully on many projects. Three stars may also mean, especially for abstract patterns, that there is a solid theoretical derivation or justification of the pattern in the literature and folklore of the subject. If there are no stars, it means that we think this is a good idea but would like people to try and see. One and two stars are interpreted on the scale between these extremes in the evident manner.

The length of our patterns varies quite a lot. Partly this reflects our knowledge and experience of the patterns and therefore our confidence in them. However, sometimes it merely reflects the fact that they are easy to describe and understand.

3.2   Getting started on your site

This section introduces the patterns that you will need when setting out on a website design project. They are organized according to the pseudo-hierarchy or graph in Figure 3.1. The patterns are numbered for the purpose of easy reference to them. They are also color-coded as described in the key.

You may also visit a (possibly updated) version of the *wu* pattern language site at www.trireme.com. We may represent the interconnections among patterns diagrammatically. The diagram in Figure 3.1 is used on the *wu* website too, as a means of navigating among the patterns. Clicking on a pattern name will take you to its description. We suggest that you read this chapter through before visiting the website.

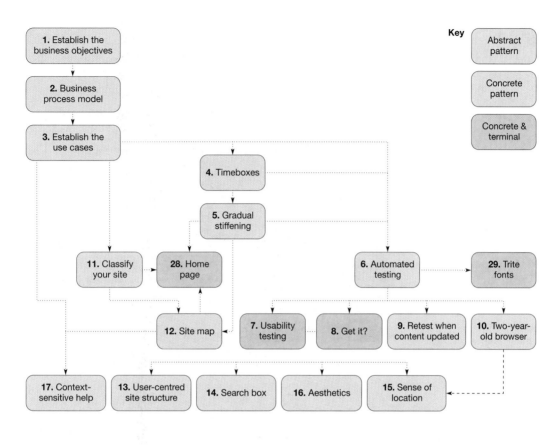

Figure 3.1

*Patterns for getting started
on a site design*

In this and subsequent diagrams, rounded rectangles represent patterns and an arrow from pattern P_1 to pattern P_2 is to be interpreted as meaning 'P_1 possibly generates a context for applying P_2 and indicates that the designer should consider applying P_2 whenever she has applied P_1'.

吴 1   Establish the business objectives ★★★

Joint requirements workshops solve many problems

You are about to create a new website or modify an existing one. The organization has a strategy, but there are possibly several stakeholders with conflicting requirements. If you do not know what they are or how to resolve these conflicts, you will almost certainly produce a site that is unfit for use.

~ ~ ~

Problem

Many people think that writing down a few use cases for the site is coextensive with understanding the requirements. Jackson (1998) has demonstrated amply that this is not so and that specification and requirements are quite different things. Furthermore, business objectives are not the same as requirements. For example, the statements 'we must double our DVD sales' and 'the site must make the DVDs more prominent than books' are quite different, though related of course.

When you decide to use **TIMEBOXES (4)** to control iterative development, you can only negotiate sensibly on evolving requirements if you have consensus on the things that will *not* change during the project.

This pattern is one of several in this book whose applicability is far wider than web design and could – no, should – be adopted usefully on non-web projects. We include it because it is as fundamental to the success of web projects as to others and because it is, in our experience, one of the patterns most often ignored by web developers – to the ultimate detriment of their projects. It is a process pattern.

Business objectives allow teams to validate their use case and business process models. How should they be discovered?

Historically, system requirements were captured from users during a series of interviews. Systems analysts would interview individual users or, sometimes, small groups of users, on an aspect of the required system. The results of these interviews would be collected into a systems analysis report, which would then be circulated for comments. Based on the comments received, a revision would be issued for further comments, and so on. Such reports were usually very large and often quite unreadable. It is difficult to believe that anyone ever both read and understood them all. One suspects that they were often signed in default of a full understanding, rather than provoke a fruitless confrontation. Other significant defects of this approach include the following:

◆ Often different stakeholders and groups will present contradictory opinions, which lead to contradictory requirements specifications. These may be uncovered later during use case modeling but are usually not noticed until the site has gone live.

◆ The approach is inclined to inculcate an 'us and them' attitude in the business and the developers. The business people ask for features and state requirements. The developers go away and produce something. What is produced rarely matches the – perhaps unarticulated – requirements exactly. Squabbling and finger-pointing follow inexorably.

A facilitated joint requirements workshop can be run to address these problems directly. Such a workshop will:

◆ ensure that all participants hear the contributions of others at first hand, which eases the problem of arriving at compromises where these are necessary;

◆ help developers gain a first-hand appreciation of the real goals of the business, as opposed to a mediated set of requirement statements;

◆ develop a shared ownership of the project between and among developers and the business;

◆ reduce the elapsed time needed to establish the requirements;

◆ establish the tempo of a rapid development process.

A workshop will focus on a particular process-oriented business area and its mission. Agree and write the mission statement for the site on a flip-chart page and place where everyone can see it – and possibly amend it as discussion proceeds. Next, the facilitator asks participants to call out and discuss the specific objectives of this site. These are written on a flip-chart. Experience has taught that there are usually about 13 objectives, either due to the fact that people run out of ideas after that much discussion, that 13 objectives comfortably fill two flip-chart pages or, as a more remote possibility, reflecting some obscure law of nature yet to be articulated by rational man. No activity should be allowed to produce a deliverable without it being tested. This principle is applied to the objectives by seeking a measure for each objective. For example, if our business is running an hotel and an objective is to provide a high-quality service, then the measure might be a star rating system as provided by many tourist boards or motoring organizations. Of course, there are cases where a precise measure is elusive. Discussing the measures is an important tool for clarifying, elucidating and completing the objectives shared and understood by the group. The discussion of measures helps a group think more clearly about the objectives and often leads to the discovery of additional ones or the modification of those already captured. Setting aside plenty of time for the discussion of the measures is seldom a waste of time.

The minimum requirement is that it must be possible to prioritize all the objectives. A formal preference grid can be elicited by asking that each pair of objectives be ranked against each other. In workshops, this is too time consuming and a quicker, more subjective technique is needed. One way to come quickly to the priorities is to allow participants to place votes against each objective. We usually permit each person a number of votes corresponding to about 66% of the number of objectives, e.g. nine votes for 13 objectives. A good way to perform the voting is to give each eligible participant a number of small, sticky, colored paper disks, of the sort that are sold in strips by most stationers. Then the rules of voting are explained: 'You may place all your stickers on one objective or distribute them across several, evenly or unevenly according to the importance you place on the objectives. You need not use all your votes; but you are not allowed to give – or sell – unused votes to other participants.' Then everyone must come up to the flip charts all at once. No hanging back to see what others do is permitted. This helps inject a dynamic atmosphere into the proceedings and stops people waiting to see what the boss does before voting.

Two rounds of voting should be done, under different interpretations, and the results added to reach a final priority score for each objective. Of course, two colors are then needed for the sticky disks. An example of two possible interpretations that can be combined is:

1 Vote from your point of view as an individual.

2 Vote from a corporate viewpoint.

Another pair might be:

1 Vote from the supplier's viewpoint.

2 Vote from the customer's viewpoint.

The results often generate further useful discussion. Also, one should allow for re-prioritization at this point if surprising results have emerged. This is often due to overlap between objectives that is highlighted by the priorities given.

An objective that cannot be measured and/or prioritized must be rejected or, at least, consigned to a slightly modified mission statement. The priorities are a key tool for project management since they determine what must be implemented first from the point of view of the business sponsor. Technical dependencies must also be allowed for, of course. Often, a discussion around these issues elicits new objectives, clarifies existing ones, or leads to their recombination or even placement in the overall mission statement. Issues that cannot be resolved are recorded with the names of the people responsible for resolving them. Specific assumptions and exclusions should also be recorded.

Priorities will be used to resolve conflicts later. They should be numerical. The Dynamic Systems Development Method (DSDM) (Stapleton, 1997) must have, should have, could have, want to have (but not in this release) (MoSCoW) ratings system will not usually work for this – every stakeholder insists that his pet objective is a Must Have.

Known uses

Detailed guidelines for organizing and running workshops can be found in Graham (2001). The technique has been used successfully on hundreds of projects around the world over ten years or so. About ten of these were web design projects.

Therefore

Hold a workshop involving as many stakeholders as possible. Make sure that potential users are represented by marketing personnel or the results of focus groups, surveys, etc. Find a good facilitator. Agree a mission statement. Find measures for each objective. Agree a numerical rank ordering of the priorities.

~ ~ ~

Each mission statement is now linked to several measurable and prioritized business objectives. We can now begin to construct a **BUSINESS PROCESS MODEL (2)** within the workshop and manage the project beyond it using **TIMEBOXES (4)**.

2

Business process model ★★

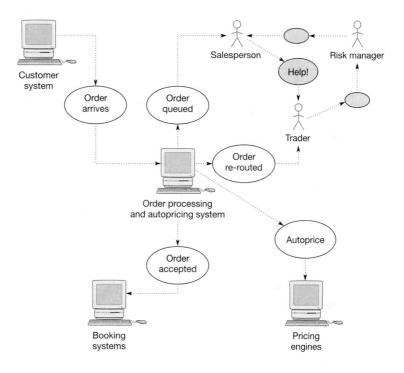

A simple business process model

You have **ESTABLISHED THE BUSINESS OBJECTIVES (1)** and prioritized them in the first sessions of a joint requirements workshop.

~ ~ ~

Problem

You now need to understand the requirements and the business processes involved, both as they are now and after the site goes live. You realize that this is different from merely specifying the use cases for the site's potential users, since many people involved (such as warehouse staff or credit-card authorizers) may never even see the site. However, you must understand their needs and activities as well as those of users.

This is another process pattern of sweeping generality but too often ignored by web developers.

The commonest misconception in computing is that understanding a client's requirements is the same as specifying a system that will meet those requirements. On such a premise, one can then blithely state that use case analysis is the only requirements modeling technique needed. Jackson (1998) pours scorn on this idea, arguing that use cases are useful for specifying systems but that they cannot describe requirements fully. Use cases connect actors, which represent **users** adopting roles, to systems. Requirements, on the other hand, may be those of people and organizations that never get anywhere near the system boundary. A requirements document must be written in a language whose designations concern things in the world in which the system is embedded (including, of course, that system). Specifications need only describe the interfaces of the system and therefore depend on different designations. The specification describes the interface of phenomena shared between the world and the system; use cases may be used to express these. The requirements model is a description over these and other phenomena in the world; it depends on both the specification *and* the world. Jackson also states that 'the customer is usually interested in effects that are felt some distance from the machine'.

Ignoring the non-user interactions can lead to us missing important re-engineering opportunities. The model above depicts a rule-based order processing and autopricing system whose aim was to take orders from customers electronically and price them automatically using various, often complex pricing engines via the corporate object request broker (ORB). The problem was that some orders were too complex or too large to admit automatic handling. These had to be looked at by a salesperson, who would of course have an interface with the 'system'. So far, so good: a rule engine would screen 'illegal' or 'handle manually' orders. The salesperson would then apply their various spreadsheet and other routines to such orders. But a further problem existed: some orders were so complicated as to be beyond the skills of the salesperson, who did not have expertise in financial mathematics. For these orders, the salesperson had to go across the office and talk to a specialist trader, who had the requisite PhD in financial engineering. We also modelled non-use-case conversations (depicted in purple) and, as a result, when our domain expert looked at the simulation we had built, she realized immediately that if we gave the trader a screen we could radically improve the workflow, and thereby the customer service. Even this relatively minor excursion away from the system boundary thus had a big cash impact. In many web applications, the importance of going beyond the boundary will be greater still.

Jackson's argument implies that we need a specific technique for modeling business processes distinct from, but compatible with, use case models of specifications. The alternative is to fall back on a veritable Russian doll of nested models described in terms of 'business use cases' (Jacobson *et al.*, 1995), an approach that is not only clumsy but also fails to address the above arguments.

Once the objectives are stated clearly with defined measures and priorities we can construct our first object model: an object model of the business area that we are dealing with. To do this, we must understand what a business (process) actually is. Most vendors of business process modeling tools and techniques find it very difficult to answer the question, 'What is a business process?' Typically, they might answer that a business is a set of processes connected by data flows, with timings for each process and (possibly) allocations of process responsibility to functional units. In other words, data flow diagrams enhanced with timings or perhaps UML activity diagrams are all that is needed. What all these approaches have in common is that they lack an adequate *theory* of what a business process is. The theory behind this pattern is rooted in the science of semiotics, and the work of Winograd and Flores (1986) on workflow systems. Rather than taking use cases as a starting point, we extract them from a process model.

Both requirements engineering and business process re-engineering must start with a model of the communications and contracts among the participants in the business and the other stakeholders, customers, suppliers, and so on.

Consider some business or enterprise. It could be an entire small company, a division or department of a larger one, or even a sole trader. A **business process** (or business area) is a network of communicating agents. Flores (1997) refers to this as a network of *commitments*. An **agent** is any entity in the world that can communicate; so it could represent a customer, regulator, employee, organizational unit, computer system, or even a mechanical device of a certain type, such as a clock. Agents are autonomous and flexible. They respond to appropriate stimuli and they can be proactive and exhibit a social aspect, i.e. communicate. Typically agents exhibit some level of intelligence, human agents certainly so but mechanical agents in so far as they can initiate and respond to communication. This now begs the question of what it means for two agents to communicate. Agents need not be site users, i.e. actors. Agents – like actors – are to be thought of as adopting a role.

This 'business' must communicate with the outside world to exist at all and, if it does so, it must use some convention of signs and signals thereto. We can call these signals between agents **semiotic acts**. They are *carried* by some material substratum. They involve a number of semiotic levels from data flows up to implicit social relationships.[1] For example, the substrate may consist of filled-in forms and the social context might be that one assumes that no practical jokes are to be played. If the substratum is verbal (or written) natural language, then we can speak instead of **speech acts** or **conversations**. These are the speech acts of Austin (1962) and Searle (1969). Flores (1997) argues that business conversations have a constant recurrent structure based on only five primitive speech acts: assert, assess, declare, offer/promise and request.

Semiotic acts (or conversations, as we will call them from now on) can be represented by messages, which are directed from the initiator (source) of the communication to its recipient (target). By *abus de langage* we can identify semiotic acts, or conversations, with their representation as messages, although strictly they are different; the same semiotic act may be represented by many different messages.[2] This defines equivalence classes of messages, and we can think of our actual message as a generic representative of its class; many contracts may express the same relationship so we choose one to represent its equivalence class.

---

[1] Semiotics is the comparative study of sign systems and has been important in such diverse fields as mathematical logic, natural language processing, anthropology and literary criticism. It holds that signs can be analyzed at at least three levels: those of syntax, semantics and pragmatics. There can be as many as five levels, up to and including the level defined by the social relations of production.

[2] For a trivial example, consider that the same conversation may be represented by a message in English, Chinese, German or Urdu.

A typical conversation is represented in Figure 3.2, where a typical external customer agent places an order with some business. This message includes the definition of the reply: {order accepted | out of stock | etc.}. We, quite legitimately, use the UML use case symbol to represent the conversation but overload the UML actor symbol to represent agents.

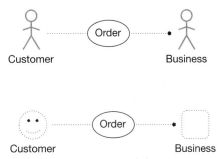

Figure 3.2

A conversation in UML

Figure 3.3

Rendering with new stereotypes

If a distinction between actors (who are users) and other agents (who are not) is required, symbols like those in Figure 3.3 can be used.

Data flow in **both** directions along message links (via the request and handover stages discussed below). This is why we have chosen to terminate message links at the recipient end with a filled circle rather than an arrowhead. The line segment is directed from the *initiator* of the communication, not from the origin of the data.

We now begin to see that agents can be modelled as objects that pass messages to each other. Clearly, agents can also be classified into different types.

We think of a business process as a network of related conversations between agents, represented by messages. It is inconceivable in most businesses that the message initiator does not wish to change the state of the world in some way as a result of the communication. This desired state of the world is the **goal** of the conversation and every conversation (or message) has a goal or post-condition, even if it is often unstated: the contract representing the conditions of satisfaction of the conversation.

A goal is achieved by the performance of a **task.** The innovation here is twofold. The tasks we perform can often be reduced to a few stereotypes: typical tasks that act as pattern matching templates against which real tasks can be evaluated and from which real tasks (or use cases) can be generated. This prevents an explosion in the number of use cases.

In business, only serious, goal-oriented conversations are relevant and therefore we can argue that each conversation has a sixfold structure as follows:

1   A **triggering event:** a world event that triggers the interaction.

2   A **goal:** a world state desired by the initiator of the conversation.

3   An **offer** or **request**, which contains the data necessary for the recipient to evaluate the offer or request.

4   A **negotiation**, whereby the recipient determines whether the goals are shared and the conditions of acceptance, leading to either a **contract** being agreed or the offer rejected. The contract formalizes the goal and provides formal conditions for knowing when the goal has been achieved satisfactorily.

5   A **task** that must be performed by the recipient of a request to achieve the goal and satisfy the contract. This is what is normally thought of as a use case when one of the agents is an actor.

6   A **handover** of the product of the task and any associated data, which checks that the conditions of satisfaction of the goals have been met.

This structure accords generally with that of a *conversation for action* in the terminology of Winograd and Flores (Flores, 1997; Winograd and Flores, 1986). Note also that there is a symmetry of offers and requests, so that we can replace every offer with an equivalent request by swapping the initiator with the recipient. Flores presents the theory in terms of a customer (our initiator) and a performer (our recipient) who executes the primitive speech acts – shown in italics in what follows. The customer *assesses* her concerns and *asserts* a request to the performer (dually the performer makes an offer). A process of negotiation then ensues, aimed at defining a contract that can be *promised* by the performer and accepted by the customer. This, and other stages in the conversation, may involve recursion, whereby subsidiary conversations are engaged in. At the end of negotiation, the contract defines the conditions of customer satisfaction, and then some task must be executed to fulfil their promise. Finally, the results of this work are *declared* complete and handed over to the customer, who should *declare* satisfaction.

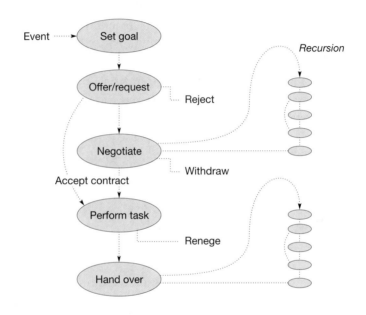

Figure 3.4

The structure of a conversation for action

Figure 3.4 shows the structure of a conversation and illustrates that recursion can occur in each segment of the conversation and that either party may withdraw at each stage.

Consider the concrete example of buying a house. An initiator might say, 'Would you like to buy my house?' and the recipient would need to know, and would negotiate on, the price. This negotiation could well involve (recursively) subsidiary conversations between the recipient and a mortgage provider and a building surveyor. If everything is agreed, then a contract will be agreed and signed (literally in this case). Now there is work to do; in England it is called conveyancing. The work involves searching local government records and land registry documents along with many other – all fairly straightforward – tasks. So this is the place where we might rely on a standard task script, as exemplified by the words (or flowcharts) in a book on conveyancing. Finally, when this task completes satisfactorily, we can hand over the keys and the contract is said to be *completed*.

Of course, in business process re-engineering, we are eager to capture not just the messages that cross the business boundary, such as order placement, but also to model the communications among our customers, suppliers, competitors, etc. This provides the opportunity to offer new services to these players, perhaps taking over their internal operations – for a fee of course.

Having analyzed the business process in terms of conversations, we now focus on the task performance segment of the conversation: the use case if actors are involved. Before doing so, let us remind ourselves of the model sequence. We started with a mission grid leading to several processes. Each process has several objectives. Also, there is now a network of conversations (messages). We should now ask two critically important questions:

◆ Does every message support the achievement of *at least one* objective?

◆ Is *every* objective supported by at least one message?

If the answer to either question is 'no', then the model must be amended. Either we have missed some conversations or we are modeling conversations that do not contribute to the achievement of any stated business objective. Of course, it is possible that we have missed an important objective and, in that case, the users should be consulted to see if the statement of objectives needs to be modified. If not, we have a clear re-engineering opportunity: just stop doing the work that supports no objective.

Known uses   This technique has been used successfully on hundreds of projects known to us around the world over ten years or so. About ten of these were web design projects.

UML provides another notation for business process modeling: the activity diagram. Our agent conversation diagrams offer a

convenient alternative to activity diagrams, which makes all implementation assumptions very explicit and, more importantly, in a
way more readily understandable by users; the activity notation is
quite hard to remember, understand and explain. Of course, there
may be occasions when activity diagrams are helpful. Martin and
Odell (1998) give the following criteria for deciding whether to use
this kind of representation. Consider using activity charts if:

◆ an object has complex, significant state (use state charts);

◆ there is complex interaction between a few objects that trigger
state changes in each other – as often found in real-time control
systems;

◆ object behavior is event driven and single threaded and objects
have only one state variable (note that business processes are
notoriously multi-threaded);

◆ the user culture supports their use – as in the telecomms sector.

Avoid them if:

◆ there are several threads (as in a typical business process);

◆ there is complex interaction between large numbers of objects;

◆ objects have several significant state variables.

Therefore   **Understand first the network of agents and commitments that make
up the business. Specify the conversations that take place at an
appropriate level of abstraction, so that they are stereotypes for actual
stories. Get people to tell these stories. Ensure that you produce both
'before' and 'after' business process models. Eliminate conversations
that do not correspond to business objectives (or discover the missed
objective). Ensure every objective is supported by a conversation.**

~ ~ ~

Now that you understand the before and after business models, it
is necessary to specify the site, so we must first **ESTABLISH THE USE
CASES (3)** at the system boundary and divide them into groups to
be delivered in individual **TIMEBOXES (4)**.

县 3   Establish the use cases ★★★

AKA

ESTABLISH THE USE CASE AND OBJECT MODELS;

UNDERSTAND USERS' TASKS FIRST;

TASK-CENTERED INFORMATION ARCHITECTURE.

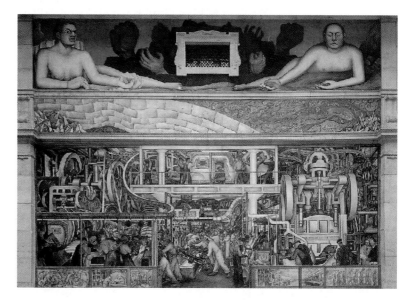

Diego Rivera, **Detroit Industry** *or* **Man and Machine, South Wall** *1932–1933 Fresco, © 2002 Banco de México Diego Rivera & Frida Kahlo Museums Trust, Av. Cinco de Mayo No. 2, Col. Centro, Del. Cuauhtémoc 06059, México, D.F. and Instituto National de Bellas Artesy Literatura.*

You have constructed a **BUSINESS PROCESS MODEL (2)** consisting of agents and conversations. This was linked to the prioritized business objectives established earlier in the workshop: **ESTABLISH THE BUSINESS OBJECTIVES (1)**.

~ ~ ~

The site must serve at least one significant business purpose. For this reason, we must look at all the use cases that we can predict users will want to execute.

This is another process pattern of sweeping generality often ignored by web developers.

It is widely believed that establishing users' tasks and responsibilities is a prerequisite for building any useful computer system. The vulgar term for this is use case analysis. Other people talk of task analysis or usage-centered design. Sometimes we need to organize these tasks into a workflow ... but ... task-centric interfaces constrain the freedom of users and inhibit their creative use of sites. How do we balance these forces?

During the construction of the business process model, we got people to tell stories and produce storyboards. Now we focus on the stories that concern people interacting directly with the site: users, maintenance staff, content managers, and so on.

How will users for example, react to our forcing them to complete **MANDATORY FIELDS (71)**; will they regard them as intrusive attacks on their privacy or an unnecessary waste of their valuable time and phone bill? How will they cope with a disabled **BACK BUTTON (35)** should we decide to disable it? More generally, how do we assure the user of a successful completion to their tasks in terms of navigating to required content or completing a workflow transaction?

Answers to these questions are only possible if you really understand who your users are and how they might interact with the site. The most common way to gain such understanding is to identify the actors (users adopting a role) that use the sites and the tasks they wish to carry out: the use cases. This is not a tutorial, on UML or object-oriented analysis but we will pause to give a brief description of the technique. For a fuller tutorial, see any of Graham (2001), Cockburn (2000) or Fowler (1997); there is an extensive tutorial based on Graham's work at www.trireme.com.

Use case modeling

The technique starts with the 'business use cases' discovered using **BUSINESS PROCESS MODEL (2)**. We now focus on the system boundary and the actors that will use the site. For each of these, we enumerate and document the use cases. There are several possible styles of doing this.

Many people fill in templates, often based on those of Cockburn. Richard Dué (private communication) recommends using a stimulus–response format. We think that a use case is best specified by writing pre- and post-conditions using a minimalist template having roughly the following form:

1 Name and description.

2 Actor(s).

3 Component use cases (if any).

4 Pre-conditions.

5 Post-condition (goal).

6 Recoverable exception use cases.

7 Fatal exception use cases.

8 Comments.

Note that we include non-functional requirements in the goal so that it is possible to state: 'the user has submitted a valid order and received confirmation in less than *n* seconds'.

As an example, consider a web-based postal lending library. There will be a use case named Borrow whose goal might be written:

The <u>member</u> has been *identified* and a <u>loan</u> *recorded* for a book.

The same <u>book</u> has been *dispatched* to the member within 8 hours and the book is no longer *in stock*.

This example shows that the use case goals provide the vocabulary for discussing the problem domain. Nouns (underlined) suggest object types and verbs (in italics) suggest associations and operations. Nothing is said about how the goal is accomplished at this stage. We must now go on to specify an object model that provides an ontology for the site.[3]

Object modeling

This is not the place for an exegesis on object modeling, even though it is an essential prerequisite to using the further patterns in this language. The technique summarized above has its origins in Catalysis (D'Souza and Wills, 1999) and is summarized in Graham (2001). For a tutorial on building use case and object models specifically in the context of web design, see Cato (2001).

---

[3] That is to say a vocabulary bound to a complete and consistent type model.

Cato seems to regard building the use cases and building the object model as separate patterns. We think these activities are linked too inextricably to do this. Thus the first alternative name given above for this pattern.

Establishing as many use cases as possible lets you think rationally about subsequent design decisions that you will make. If the priorities are carried over from the business process model, they will turn into a valuable tool for managing projects using **TIME-BOXES (4)**. They also form a sound and invaluable basis for the testing patterns that we will meet later.

Known uses   Use case modeling is a well-established technique for systems development and is part of most mainstream methods for object-oriented and component-based development. This applies equally to object modeling using UML as a notation.

Therefore   Extract the use cases from the conversations in the **BUSINESS PROCESS MODEL (2)**. Record their correspondences to the business objectives. Write post-conditions for each use case. Compare the vocabulary of the post-conditions to the type model. Write use cases in stimulus–response form. Convert the use cases into the user training manual and the test plan. Develop **CONTEXT-SENSITIVE HELP (17)** from them. One stimulus–response pair from the use case should correspond to one step in the workflow if the site deals with workflows. If not, do not constrain the user's ability to perform steps in any particular sequence. Ensure that you extract and document a business object type model from the use case goals.

~ ~ ~

You must now **CLASSIFY YOUR SITE (11)**. One reason is to establish whether it must enforce workflows. Use a **SITE MAP (12)** and for workflow sites **CONTEXT-SENSITIVE HELP (17)** to help the user complete use cases according to the constraints set by the organization and the needs of the user. Use the use cases as the basis to **AUTOMATE TESTING (6)**.

昊 4   Timeboxes ★★★

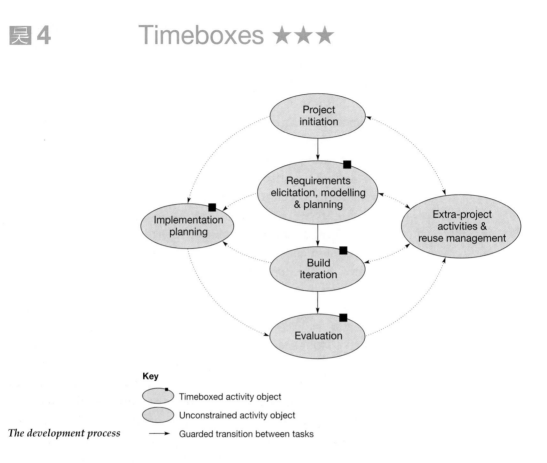

Key

⬭• Timeboxed activity object

⬭ Unconstrained activity object

The development process ⟶ Guarded transition between tasks

You have completed a **BUSINESS PROCESS MODEL (2)**, a use case model and begun to extract a type model. Now you have to ensure timely delivery of a site that meets current requirements as closely as possible.

~ ~ ~

Problem   **Time pressure fights against both robustness and the need to respond to changing business requirements during the project. However, timely delivery is nearly always a critical success factor.**

This is another process pattern of great generality sometimes ignored by web developers.

Rapid application development (RAD), as a development approach, began to be popular in the late 1980s but its origins remain obscure. The Joint Application Development (JAD) workshop technique used at IBM was certainly an influential component. Rapid prototyping had been used for years and also penetrated the RAD approach. James Martin is sometimes accused of first coining the phrase, but the earliest formal declaration seems to be the Ripp (rapid iterative production prototyping) method developed at El du Pont de Nemours and promoted later at a conference under the slogan: 'Your system in 128 days – or your money back'. Ripp was followed by many proprietary imitations and soon every consultancy had its own version and name. What they all had in common is the use of workshops and timeboxes. A timebox sets a rigid limit to prototype iterations to ensure management control over prototyping. A small team is mandatory and the tested prototype is both end point and deliverable. RAD methods vary in the extent to which users participate in the prototyping process and the kind of tools used. This pattern emphasizes building a bridge between the understanding of the business people and the developers, and integrating their effort.

The timebox technique offers the following benefits. It imposes management control over ripple effects and uncontrolled iteration. Control is achieved by setting a rigid elapsed time limit on the iterations and using a small project team. Furthermore, it has a usable system as both the endpoint of the process and its deliverable. There is no distinction between production, evolution and maintenance as with conventional approaches, which usually ignore maintenance costs during project justification.

Timeboxes tackle the following management issues:

◆ Wants *versus* needs – by forcing requirements to be prioritized by negotiation between users and developers. Users and the project team are forced to concentrate on the real needs of the business.

◆ Creeping functionality – in the traditional lifecycle, the long delay between specification and delivery can lead to users requesting extra features. The use of a time limit reduces this tendency.

◆ Project team motivation – the developers can see a tangible result of their efforts emerging.

◆ The involvement of stakeholders at every stage reduces implementation shock.

The approach reduces time to market, not by a magic trick that makes hard things easy but by delivering an important usable subset of the entire system in no more than a few weeks.

It is absolutely critical to maintain credibility; build on success and manage expectations during the process. This is achieved by several means. Customers should be warned that a quickly developed prototype may conceal much complexity. A working site will take time in proportion to the complexity of the tasks it assists with. You will know what these are because you **ESTABLISHED THE USE CASES (3)**. Equally, customers should be stimulated by many small, incremental deliveries. We have **ESTABLISHED THE BUSINESS OBJECTIVES (1)** and prioritized them so that developers can show that corners that are cut to keep within time limits are low-priority corners. Developers can thus afford to accept reasonable changes to requirements, provided that existing, low priority requirements can be eliminated by mutual agreement based on the priorities. This expectation management is a key task for the project manager. If it is neglected, the project will usually fail.

This technique prevents paralysis by analysis, errors due to delay, spurious requirements and implementation shock. It usually motivates teams better than the waterfall approach.

The DSDM is a 'framework of controls for rapid application development' (Stapleton, 1997). There are no prescribed techniques. DSDM has a rudimentary and high-level process model that can be tailored for individual organizations' requirements. It was developed as a potentially standard approach by a consortium of 17 British user organizations in 1994 that now has over 1000 members world-wide. DSDM has nine fundamental principles, all of which the process described below adheres to totally. They are:

1 Active user involvement is imperative.

2 Teams are empowered to make decisions.

3 The focus is on the frequent delivery of products.

4 Fitness for business purpose is the essential criterion for acceptance of deliverables.

5 Iterative development and incremental delivery are necessary to converge on an accurate business solution.

6   All changes during development are reversible.

7   Requirements are defined at a high level.

8   Testing is integrated throughout the lifecycle.

9   A collaborative and co-operative approach between all stakeholders is essential.

These principles enable an organization to determine whether a particular project is suitable for the approach. For example, if you know perfectly well that under no circumstances will a sample of (at least surrogate) users be available, then forget it.

What DSDM does give is a framework that can be informed with the concrete political and organizational characteristics of a project. The commitment to timeboxing (principle 3) means that milestones are equated with deliverables, making the approach very product oriented. Testing is performed throughout the lifecycle, rather than as an end-stage activity, and this leads to far higher quality and far fewer implementation surprises. Very importantly, the products and documentation mandated by DSDM are as minimal as possible, while still ensuring adequate quality and progress towards delivery and maintenance.

One useful contribution from DSDM (suggested first by Dai Clegg of Oracle, I understand) parallels the prioritization of objectives in SOMA workshops. DSDM classifies requirements into must have, should have, could have and want to have (but not in this release). This categorization is referred to by the contraction MoSCoW. However, several recent experiences have shown that there is a tendency for every stakeholder to insist that their pet requirement is a must. To counter this, we recommend a numerical prioritization based on consensus if possible. The voting technique described in **ESTABLISH THE BUSINESS OBJECTIVES (1)** is one way to achieve this. If (much) more time is available, pairwise ranking may be a more 'scientific' approach.

The prioritized use cases provide perhaps the only rational basis for negotiation with stakeholders when deadlines slip or requirements evolve. Fix the business objectives and priorities for the duration of each project but allow the requirements to evolve. Drop the use cases and types corresponding to the lowest-priority objectives where technically possible.

Look for quick wins. For example, when testing your site there will be instances when a tester hits a problem that surprises the developers but for which the solution is obvious. In a similar category are fixes that require little or no effort or those where a small effort will have a big impact. It is important to give such fixes a high priority and de-scope other features accordingly.

Therefore

Divide the use cases into coherent groups, taking into account technical constraints (e.g. client–server dependencies, supplier lead times, etc.) and business issues (e.g. unitary business offering). There are three possibilities:

1   **Tackle the easiest area first to boost developers' confidence.**

2   **Tackle the area that solves 80% of the business need first.**

3   **Tackle the area with the greatest technical challenge first.**

The first approach is seldom the right one, because there can be some nasty shocks awaiting the team downstream and because it is not a good way to impress users with the team's skills. A combination of the other two approaches is ideal. The focus too is on the essential requirements early on, rather than those features that the business (or the developers) would like the system to have ideally.

Set definite delivery dates for the software and content that implement each such group of use cases. When deadlines seem endangered, cut functionality instead. But don't expect to get all the requirements right first time. If stakeholders request new or changed functionality, rate its importance against the prioritized business objectives. Negotiate on what must be deferred to the next timebox if the new features are to be included. Drop use case functionality corresponding to the lowest-priority objectives. Never deliver late. Don't compromise on quality unless there is an argument to do so based on the objectives. Don't allow anyone to change the objectives or their priorities.

~ ~ ~

Now begin to develop the site using **GRADUAL STIFFENING (5)**. **AUTOMATE TESTING (6)** wherever possible. Start **USABILITY TESTING (7)** early on. Use **GET-IT? (8)** tests as soon as possible too.

昃 5   Gradual stiffening ★★

AKA   **AGILE PROCESS, EXTREME PROGRAMMING**

The alternative to sudden collapse, reproduced courtesy of www.wheelsofindustry .com

You are managing the project using the discipline of **TIMEBOXES (4)** and you have **ESTABLISHED THE USE CASES (3)** in the context of a **BUSINESS PROCESS MODEL (2)** and a set of fixed, prioritized objectives. However ...

~ ~ ~

Problem   The requirements and use cases may evolve during the lifetime of the project. How do you respond to such developments? Should you adhere strictly to the original plan? If not, what is fixed and what should be allowed to vary?

This is a process pattern of general applicability. It is a very, very minor modification of the one due to Alexander *et al.* (1997, pp. 963–9). They recommend the following procedure for building houses

The fundamental philosophy behind the use of pattern languages is that buildings should be uniquely adapted to individual needs and sites; and that the plans of buildings should be rather loose and fluid, in order to accommodate these subtleties ...

Recognize that you are not assembling a building from components like an erector set, but that you are instead weaving a structure which starts out globally complete, but flimsy; then gradually making it stiffer but still rather flimsy; and only finally making it completely stiff and strong.

In the description of this pattern, the reader is invited to visualize a 50-year-old master carpenter at work. He keeps working, apparently without stopping, until he eventually produces a quality product. The smoothness of his labor comes from the fact that he is making small, sequential, incremental steps such that he can always eliminate a mistake or correct an imperfection with the next step. He compares this with the novice who with a 'panic-stricken attention to detail' tries to work out everything in advance, fearful of making an unrecoverable error. Alexander's point is that most modern architecture has the character of the novice's work, not the master craftsman's. Successful construction processes, producing well-fitting forms, come from the postponement of detailed design decisions until the building process itself so that the details are fitted into the overall, evolving structure. Another characterization of the process talks about visiting the site *with the client* and, after discussion, just placing stakes where the corners of the house will be and heavy stones to mark the entrance and perhaps windows. Detailed decisions, such as where to channel the electrics, will be made much later in the project by the appropriate craftsmen – again in constant consultation with the client.

We think that software and website design should be like that too. It is also a stance remarkably similar to that taken by the proponents of eXtreme programming.

Beck (2000) introduced the set of ideas called eXtreme Programming (XP), a method that emphasizes frequent delivery of tangible, working results. Beck called the approach 'extreme' because it attempts to take commonplace good ideas and apply them aggressively. For example, as he puts it:

◆ If code reviews are good, review code all the time (pair programming).

◆ If short iterations are good, make them *really* short (hours not months).

◆ If testing is good, then everyone tests all the time.

◆ If simplicity is good, then build the simplest thing that could work.

It is an implicit principle of XP that one should listen to the business all the time. However, some particularly extreme advocates of XP take this to mean that there is no need to establish the requirements before coding: 'All that matters is the code!' These people take the view that if you get it wrong you can change the code easily, so why bother. This is wrong for two reasons. First, misunderstood requirements may not bite until the development team has moved on to other projects. Second, it is hard to believe Beck when he tells us that developers with 'ordinary skills' can make it work – contradicting Alexander's view on the craft nature of good design incidentally. Take the example of a very widely reported success story for XP – at Chrysler. In this case, there were very considerably talented people on the team (including Beck himself). Furthermore, the project followed on from an earlier, failed project and many of the team from that project were used. It is inconceivable to me that these very experienced people did not have a good grasp of what the requirements were before the project started. XP is an excellent way of building systems and all its techniques are useful. However, it must be accompanied (not necessarily preceded) by sound requirements engineering techniques. Another important and useful technique advocated (though not invented) by XP is pair programming. The idea is that no one person ever writes code or designs alone. One person sits and develops while another watches, thinks and comments. The two then swap around. Furthermore, the pairs are not permanent and anyone may (and will) alter someone else's code. This sounds as though it should halve productivity but, curiously, all the studies that have been done indicate that productivity doubles – or better. There may be some doubt if this will work on very large projects of course.

Taking the core ideas from XP and the patterns we have already encountered suggests the following iterative approach to site development:

1 Write tests based on the use cases.

2 Write the minimum HTML and other code to pass the tests.

3 Deliver the site to **USABILITY TESTING (7)**.

4 Release the site and solicit feedback.

5 Modify the tests as necessary.

6 Refactor the code and add new features.

7 Go to step 2.

Remember that the business objectives and priorities must remain fixed points, however.

This process starts at the lowest level, that addressed directly by XP, with coding. An agile process will almost certainly benefit from extreme ideas at this level. The good ideas include the above process, hinted at in Figure 3.5: write tests based on use cases, write the minimum code to pass the tests (perhaps working in pairs – but you don't have to), check the code in and run the automatic test harness (this is essential), run usability tests (this is forgotten by most XPers), review with the user(s), refactor, and iterate. Agility implies that this is done in very short cycles, perhaps measured in days.

Such an approach implies that the team has mastered good specification and design techniques, perhaps such as those of Catalysis (D'Souza and Wills, 1999) or UML Components (Cheesman and Daniels, 2000) for more complex server side projects. It also implies that sound refactoring methods are fully understood. The team will have read and absorbed the techniques in, say, Martin Fowler's (1999) excellent book on the subject. However, in a COM or Java world, refactoring implies a lengthy build cycle. Suppose that the change affects a complex web service offering or, worse still, an application deployed on a mobile device. Users may not be prepared to tolerate the delay or service interruption. In an interesting development MetaDyne (www.metadyne.uk.com) has shown how to address this problem and really make XP work in such situations. They have found and patented a way of doing Smalltalk-like dynamic binding in a distributed Java environment, so that (if well-designed to start with) incremental changes can be downloaded as separate components without taking the application offline. I'm afraid that without this kind of technology, XP will probably remain a minority pastime: the province of top-class developers only.

Leaving aside the issues surrounding refactoring, responding to user reviews implies a readiness to embrace any changes requested. How can this be managed without deadlines slipping? Here we get to the stuff that the more ostrich-like XPers can't see. DSDM, in common with most iterative processes, imposes project discipline with time-boxes (and other consequences of its nine principles). This strategy implies that the development team has to negotiate with its customer about which features will be dropped in order to accommodate the requested changes. DSDM recommends that its MoSCoW classification of features is the basis of such negotiations, although many or our clients have faced difficulties in trying to convince users that any requirement isn't an M (must have), as we have already pointed out. We prefer a numerical ranking. But what do you rank: use cases? Clearly not, because the review will often reveal new and changed use cases as businesses evolve.

There must be some fixed points to base the negotiation on. In the first place, we can regard the specification as fixed during very rapid cycles of a day or two. But some reviews will imply changes to the spec. The specification should therefore evolve at a slower pace, perhaps in two-week cycles. But still we need fixed points for the duration of an entire project, otherwise the timebox discipline will fail utterly.

Our solution has been to fix absolutely the business objectives and their relative priorities at the outset of projects: changed objectives imply a new project. This suggests a much slower iteration rate of perhaps six months or more. Note that hardly any

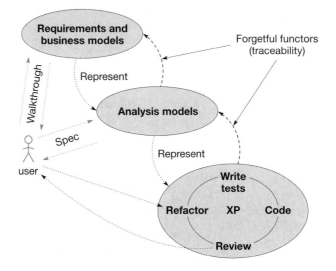

Figure 3.5

Iteration speeds up with representation

published method says anything about these business objectives. In RUP they are subsumed in a 'visioning' statement and are given no particular structure. The very phrase 'use case driven' suggests that the use cases are the starting point. No! Business objectives are the key fixed point in any project. Of course they are related to the use cases in the sense that a use case may support one or more objectives (if it doesn't, you're doing something very wrong!) but they are quite different in kind from use cases.

If you think about the process in Figure 3.5 as a mathematician might for a moment, you will see that speed of iteration increases in proportion to the tightness of the representation. A business objectives and use cases model can lead to many specifications. A specification can be designed and coded in many ways, giving what mathematicians call a 'representation'. The transformation from loose to tight representation is characterized as the selection of a representation 'functor'. In mathematics, every representation functor has an adjoint 'forgetful' functor, which literally 'forgets' the details of a particular implementation but preserves the invariants of the specification. If you're not a mathematician, ignore the jargon; this is just a metaphor. But it does provide a framework for the management of iteration and emphasizes the role of traceability in a good process.

Therefore

A website development project should start with loose design but clear business objectives, defined use cases and types and a sound project plan. Allow the site structure to stiffen the design only as the site unfolds and only completely towards the end of the project. Follow something like the seven-step iterative process suggested above. Stick to the timebox plan already agreed.

~ ~ ~

Draw an outline **SITE MAP (12)** and ensure that it conforms to the type model. Create a nice **HOME PAGE (28)**. **USER-CENTERED SITE STRUCTURE (13)** is also indicated.

Contributors and sources

Frank Buschmann, Kevin Henney, Nora Koch, Oliver Vogel, Uwe Zdun.

图 6   Automate testing ★★★

*Image reproduced with
the permission of
Dorling Kindersley*

You are using **TIMEBOXES (4)** and **GRADUAL STIFFENING (5)** to
manage the project.

~ ~ ~

Problem   This means frequent changes and refactoring of code and design.
How do you control the costs of such changes while maintaining
quality and usability?

This is another process pattern that could apply equally well to
non-web projects.

It is a principle of XP that if testing is good, then everyone should test all the time. XP is thus said to be test-driven and defines simplicity as 'just enough code to make all the tests work'. Unit tests and key-task tests should be based on known use cases. XP also uses the output from its short cycles to refactor code. Examples of refactoring include creating a superclass to abstract common features, creating new plug-points, splitting classes or methods into two, and renaming components to be more descriptive. Refactoring HTML might involve introducing cascading style sheets, removing frames, changing the **SITE MAP (12)** or changing the navigation. Doing all these things frequently relies on the presence of automated testing tools, of course.

Fowler (1999) describes well the techniques necessary for refactoring code. Dynamic binding technology, like that supplied by MetaDyne, makes refactoring in real time possible.

For regression testing, a number of tools are available. There are now some products that automate stress testing such as SafeTest (www.attenda.com). For Java work, many companies currently use Junit for unit testing and Ant (which I understand is free) for integration tests. Junit and Ant are described well at www-106.ibm.com /developerworks/library/j-ant/.

Therefore

Refactor continuously. Use automated test tools wherever possible. Make sure that you apply the tests to all browsers that might be used, including TWO-YEAR-OLD BROWSER (10) versions for public sites. Retest at every incremental change to the code or layout and RETEST WHEN CONTENT UPDATED (9).

~ ~ ~

You just cannot test things like left/right button usage consistency or many other aspects of usability automatically. Therefore do **USABILITY TESTING (7)** and **GET-IT? (8)** tests early in the project and after each significant refactoring.

7   Usability testing ★★

Our users are always thinking up new ways of testing the product!

You have built a version of the site and completed some **AUTO-MATED TESTING (6)** and perhaps tested against **TWO-YEAR-OLD BROWSERS (10)**. You have **ESTABLISHED THE USE CASES (3)** and you understand the object model.

~ ~ ~

Problem

You just cannot test things like the consistency of left/right mouse button usage, **USE OF COLOR (53)** or many other aspects of usability automatically.

The first part of usability testing is based on the use cases. Users must be able to perform all key tasks successfully and without frustration, long delays or using tortuous navigation around the site. The use cases help to define scripts for this kind of test. The tests have a dual aspect: did the user accomplish the task, and did they find it easy and pleasurable to do so?

Focus groups may be useful before you begin design. They will help to establish objectives and use cases but they are no substitute for usability testing. You can start the latter as soon as you have even an outline design in the form of hand-drawn screen mock-ups or storyboards. Usability testing should then continue throughout development. If you do it at the end of the project, it will be too late to fix the defects that it uncovers.

Remember **KISS (38)** – resist the urge to add features, such as help messages and explanations, in response to testers' comments. Instead, try to remove features that might have confused or distracted the users. If possible, simplify the navigation using the appropriate patterns downstream from this one.

If the testers were able to get back on track easily after making an error, then the cost of fixing it may not be worthwhile. Fix it only if it is easy to do so.

Change manage requests for new features as you would in any software development project, i.e. make sure there is a justifiable benefit.

Video the test sessions to record both what was on the screen and the users' actions. Record users' comments and try not to lead. Ask open questions (questions that can't be answered with a yes or a no). Record comments. Let the developers watch – possibly on a screen in a nearby room – but don't let them interfere, criticize, help or explain.

Obviously, it is better to test with real users rather than or as well as surrogate ones. Unfortunately, for websites it is very rare even to be able to know who they are, never mind test with them. When all else fails, technology can come to the rescue. Prophet (www.speed-trap.com) is a product that enables site designers to observe the actual behavior of users as they visit the site. Prophet works by downloading an applet to the browser of every visitor.

This applet then monitors the users' mouse movements and clicks and keyboard operations. This delivers a vast amount of information about usability – albeit indirectly. Consider, for example, a user filling in a form. If they spend an average of one second typing into each field but pause over the fifth one for 40 seconds, then one could infer that they have had to leave their desk to retrieve some piece of information asked for: a possible usability problem. Or do they get as far as the home page and just go away: a definite usability problem. If they move around the site a lot, you might be able to infer that they are confused by the navigation. Prophet is therefore a great way of magnifying knowledge about a site's usability – although it is not a substitute for tests.

Speed-trap insists that its customers display a privacy notice to permit the user to refuse the download. However, the information it gathers is entirely anonymous and the applet, being pure Java, cannot see what the user is doing outside the browser window. Therefore, one would hope that most users would find this monitoring acceptable. Speed-trap estimates that their system misses about 20% of users either because they demur or because they have Java disabled or use an old browser version.

Rainassure from Rainfinity is another product that can monitor transactions on e-commerce sites but runs on the server and supplies less usability data, although it does spot transaction failures that could provide some clues. One news site (telegraph.co.uk) uses a company called Whitecross to track user behavior off-line. The information is used mainly for audience analysis but, again, could provide some clues as to usability.

This pattern conceals much complexity and there is a great deal more to say about usability testing of websites. There could well be an entire pattern language for this topic. Useful sources to consult further include Lindgaard (1994), Cato (2001), Krug (2000) and van Duyne *et al.* (2002).

Therefore   **Consider hiring a usability consultant from outside the organization to avoid personality or political conflicts. Perform usability tests from the first prototype continuously throughout the project. Do not confuse usability tests with output from focus groups. If**

formal, lab-based tests are not within the budget, then test informally with the developers as *silent* observers. If you can't get real users, grab people 'off the street' or from other departments or offices. Video the session if possible. Ask people to think out loud as they use the site. Record their comments. First ask them to browse and react unprompted, then give them tasks based on the use cases. Record their successes and failures. Ask them if they're happy as a result of visiting the site – and why. Reward them for their trouble and ask if they would help in future. Don't forget to test on dial-up lines or under conditions that simulate them accurately. Use automated tools such as Prophet to enhance your understanding of how users behave.

~ ~ ~

Although there is much more to learn about the topic of usability testing, this pattern is terminal within this language. However, make sure you also do **GET-IT? (8)** testing in parallel with this pattern.

Contributors and sources   Frank Buschmann, Kevlin Henney, Nora Koch, Oliver Vogel, Uwe Zdun.

8 Get-it? ★★

You are testing your website for usability and have completed **AUTOMATED TESTING (6)** and may have begun **USABILITY TESTING (7)**.

~ ~ ~

Problem

Full usability testing using with large numbers of users or in laboratory conditions can be very expensive and time consuming: thus affecting timely update to the site. However, we must only deliver tested, usable sites.

This is a very simple pattern taken from Krug (2000). He suggests taking almost anyone that happens to be around, preferably the same kinds of people that might be users, and asking them to sit down and use the new, partly tested site. Then just ask them if they get it.

Remember that the best testers are not always the most co-operative personalities. The best ones are the cussed, impatient ones who are just too busy to play. Remember too that developers *always* want to play!

The sort of responses to be interested in include *inter alia* statements about:

- the value proposition;

- what the organization does;

- what makes them different from other organizations in the same or similar businesses;

- the purpose of the site;

- what it contains;

- how it is organized

- what could someone gain from a visit;

- whether the experience a pleasant one;

- how this site compares with other sites;

- the look and feel.

Krug distinguishes get-it? tests from key-task tests, which are based on the use cases that we know about during **USABILITY TESTING (7)**. We should also distinguish them from the regression tests carried out when we **AUTOMATE TESTING (6)** when content is updated and tests across different browsers, including **TWO-YEAR-OLD BROWSERS (10)**.

The cost of this kind of test is not prohibitive (*cf.* Tognazzini, 1992). Therefore you can afford to do it frequently. The payback is usually well worth it.

As with usability tests, do this early in the project and continuously throughout it. If tests are performed at the end, then it will be too late to fix problems before the scheduled release date.

Therefore   Use anyone available as testers if real users are not available. Explain nothing in advance. Ask them: 'Do you get it?' Ask other suitable open questions, perhaps based on the list above. Allow testers to comment freely. Use get-it? throughout the lifecycle from planning to the first released version. If testing is good, then do it all the time. If possible, use some people who have never used the web before. Let then access the site from home as well as your offices. Offer them a reasonable payment for their time. Keep the test sessions down to less than an hour.

~ ~ ~

This pattern is terminal within this language. However, make sure you also do **USABILITY TESTING (7)** in parallel with this pattern.

Contributors and sources

Krug (2000).
Tognazzini (1992).

 9

Retest when content updated ★

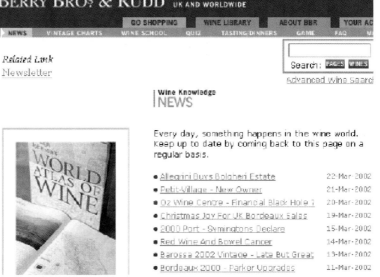

www.bbr.com

You have adopted **AUTOMATED TESTING (6)** but the content of your site will evolve inexorably. You completed **USABILITY TESTING (7)** and **GET-IT? (8)** tests before the site went live.

~ ~ ~

Problem

When content changes, there may be unintended side effects that impact upon usability even when the code that is the site has not itself changed.

Some kinds of content change may have no effect on usability but it is difficult to be sure of this unless you test every time the content changes.

When content changes frequently, as in the stock of a wine merchant, this pattern is particularly important.

Therefore

Maintain two sites: one for testing and one for the public. Run usability tests as well as the automated tests against the test site whenever content is updated. If the tests are passed, only then transfer the new version to the live site.

~ ~ ~

To ease regression testing, ensure that you **STORE CONTENT IN A DATABASE (64)**.

昙 10   Two-year-old browser ★★

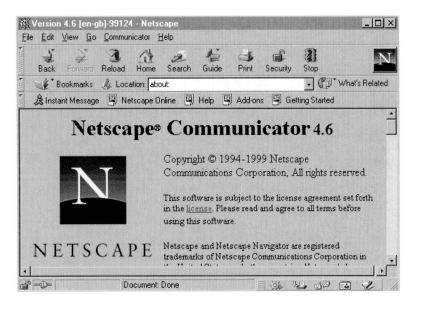

*Image © 2002 Netscape
Communications
Corporation.*

Your site is public. You are using tools to **AUTOMATE TESTING (6).**
You want as many people as possible to be able to access your site
and use all its features. However ...

~ ~ ~

Problem

Many users do not have the latest software and have underpowered
hardware. Browsers vary widely in what they support: Javascript,
plug-ins, flash, frames, etc. One browser even exhibits this
variability from version to version. To make this worse, using recent
features on underpowered hardware may lead to unacceptable
response times.

This pattern applies only to public sites since intranet users can be
provided with a known set of browsers by their employers.
     Nielsen (2000) recommends that you keep a collection of all the
major versions, of all well-known browsers for test purposes.

It is fairly easy to discover statistics on which browsers people are actually using from the web logs. However, these statistics do not guarantee that a different browser won't be used by someone tomorrow. Better to be safe than sorry!

Therefore

Test your pages against all versions of all known browsers in versions up to two years old. Repeat the tests on ten-year-old hardware. AUTOMATE TESTING (6) of this kind where possible.

~ ~ ~

As a consequence of this phenomenon, there should be **NO FRAMES ON PUBLIC SITES (27)**.

Contributors and sources

Nielsen (2000).

昊 11   Classify your site ★★

AKA   **SITE GENRES**

	STATELESS All users see the same pages. No 'process'	STATIVE Users see different content Users undertake a process
STATIC HTML,File system	Small sites	mailto:
DYNAMIC Database,XML	BBC, CNN (News), Microsoft (downloading patches) Amazon (viewing titles)	Hotmail Amazon (ordering)

You have **ESTABLISHED THE USE CASES (3)**, which will tell you a lot about how users will interact with the site. You have also built an object model that will tell you about the site's content. Now you have to design it.

~ ~ ~

Problem   **Not all the patterns in this pattern language are appropriate for all sites and situations. How does one select suitable patterns? Equally, not all layout styles work for all kinds of sites. How can one draw attention to this and standardize on an approach?**

The table above shows a basic classification scheme for websites.

Workflow sites are distinguishable from exploration sites. They are clearly dynamic and stative. Occasionally, apparently stateless sites (like news sites) take the user into a stative mode. For example, one used to be able to view and download recent crosswords from www.thetimes.com. But *The Times* started a crossword club in

June 2001, which meant that one could only get access by filling in a form to set up a password.

Different kinds of site require different navigation schemes, different graphic design and different use of language. Sites intended for children need to allow for their abilities and preferences. News sites usually adopt magazine style layouts and this seems to work. Artistic sites can get away with flashier designs and even the slightly slower download times that result than news or e-commerce sites.

Van Duyne *et al.* (2002) offer a group of patterns, which they call site genres, each concerned with one of the following kinds of site and emphasizing the different forces at work:

◆ **Arts and entertainment sites** must stimulate the eye and mind, encourage exploration and take the visitor beyond normality; users may therefore tolerate slower performance.

◆ **Community clusters** provide a means for people to meet and chat, but there is a cost associated with managing the contributions; people don't like censorship either.

◆ **Company sites** vary greatly; is the site to be used for product information, branding, sales, or what?

◆ **Educational forums** may offer online courses or learning and research tools and resources.

◆ **Enabling intranets** can help staff to communicate or enforce/ enable workflow; the site may be an educational forum too.

◆ **Government sites** provide information on policy and legislation and may enable users to submit data such as tax returns.

◆ **Grassroots information sites** cover everything from individuals' wacky hobbies to national liberation movements.

◆ **News sites** provide some stories up front and allow users to search for others. They are usually designed to look like magazines or newspapers.

◆ **Non-profit help networks** here the different types of user are the obvious challenge: staff, sufferers, volunteers, donors, etc.

◆ **Personal e-commerce sites** are the standard B2C sites.

◆ **Web services and applications**.

One might wish to add B2B to the list, but it appears fairly comprehensive otherwise. Note that there is a lot of overlap. However, making this kind of preliminary classification will help you think about the design. The more general classification given above can then be used in a more informed way.

Therefore

Before making major design decisions, first classify the site. Look at other sites of the same type and note what they have in common and how they differ from sites classified differently.

~ ~ ~

Use your **HOME PAGE (28)** to tell users what kind of site they have arrived at and what's expected of them. Construct a **SITE MAP (12)** as part of your early design. If there is a workflow or form-filling aspect to the site, make sure that you avoid **PARANOID SECURITY (74)**.

Contributors
and sources

Richard Dué.
Gareth Sylvester-Bradley.
Van Duyne *et al.* (2002).

12   Site map ★★★

AKA   **HIERARCHICAL SITE MAP**
             WORKFLOW OVERVIEW

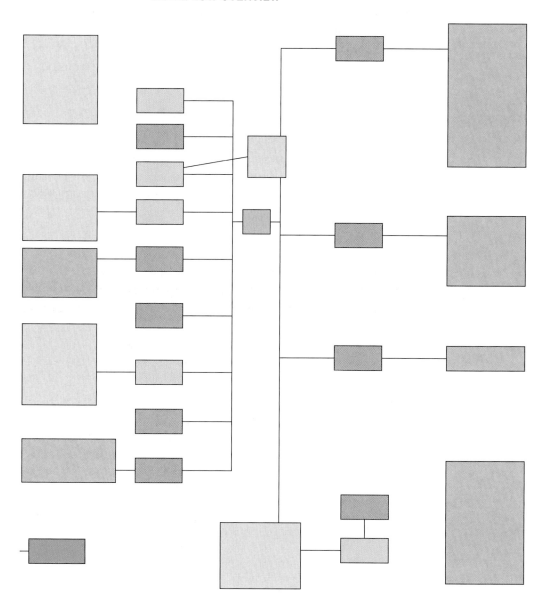

You are at the beginning of designing the site and have adopted the philosophy of **GRADUAL STIFFENING (5)** and **ESTABLISHED THE USE CASES (3)**. You have probably already used the latter to design a scheme of **CONTEXT-SENSITIVE HELP (17).** You now start to consider what the site will contain and how users will navigate around it and discover the content that they are looking for. You therefore first need to establish the outline structure of the site and the key elements of its content.

~ ~ ~

Problem

You need a convenient way to describe and think about the site's structure.

But it's not only you who needs to understand the topology of the site. Users get lost easily. They may know the location of the content they want to go to, but not how to get there. The user usually needs a contextual overview of (a) the site and its content and (b) the actions involved in any workflow that they may engage in.

A map is a useful and familiar way for people to find their way around unknown territory. Using a map, people can repair procedures that fail due to obstructions that have appeared since the procedure was created.

When we come to the detailed patterns concerning navigation, we will need a site map to organize our thoughts and solutions around.

One of the ways you might present the site map is to include a topic path in the navigation bar. This presents the current location in the hierarchical structure but fails to show cross-links or alternative paths. In the example below, you cannot tell that it is possible to reach the same destination from Sportswear.

<u>Home</u>>Men's fashion>Underwear>Jock straps

Where the site is hierarchical, the topic path can become the page's headline.

Usually, spatially organized maps are better than textually oriented ones because of transfer effects: people are used to using charts for navigation about the real world.

The site map should show all the site, not just what is linked to the home page, so that the visitor can get at all the content. If it is large, then segment it, as we have done with the *wu* site: represented in this book by the four diagrams at the start of each section of this chapter.

Veen (2001) identifies four ways in which the site map may be accessed via a navigation scheme: as a matrix, as a tree or strict hierarchy, as a set of segmented trees with cross-references, or by using a combination of these approaches.

The matrix approach, which you can see at portal sites such as yahoo.com, classifies every page according to two or more sets of keywords, the later being fixed in advance. For example, if there are to be only two sets – called services and content – we might end up with an organization like that shown in Figure 3.6.

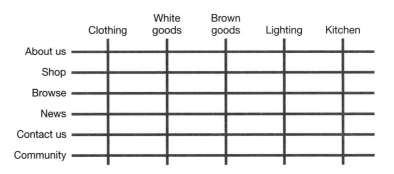

Figure 3.6

Matrix organization

Where the headings intersect, there may be a page classified accordingly, e.g. a page concerning radios for sale might be classified as Shop/Brown goods. This organization permits many ways of navigating. For example, if we have a third dimension defined by the set {dirt cheap, average, outrageously priced}, then we might offer a selection of pages based on radio buttons or pull-down menus (combo boxes). For a discussion of this, see **CONTEXT-DEPENDENT SEARCH CATEGORIES (63)**. Matrix organization can also be mapped directly on to a **THREE-REGION LAYOUT (26)**.

This example already shows a weakness of matrix organization: why did we not classify our radios under Browse? You have to be very careful in defining the headings to avoid this problem.

Most portals use an approach that combines this organization with hierarchical views. A pure hierarchical view is nearly always too restrictive, e.g. snap.com.

We think that the organization should follow the structure of the content and the use cases as far as possible. The most general organization is also the most powerful: a network. However, a completely general network can be very hard to understand. The *wu* site started off as a network but we soon realized that a hierarchical organization would make it far easier to use. Doing this proved to be the hardest bit in writing this book – and we had to compromise but some of the knowledge is just not hierarchical; thus the pseudo-hierarchical organization that we have adopted seems to be the right organization for this material and its intended use.

This pattern is related to Tidwell's **NAVIGABLE SPACES**.

Therefore

Create a graphic representing the structure of the site (usually a hierarchy). Use it to discuss the site with the team. Make it available to the site users as well. Always provide a single page that gives a visual and textual representation or overview of the entire site. Allow users to navigate directly from this representation. Icons should pop up a preview of the content to be visited using THE RHETORIC OF ARRIVAL AND DEPARTURE (20).

For workflow sites, provide an overview of the workflows based on the use cases. Consider enhancing the site map by providing an index as well (www.adobe.com provides a paradigm for this).

~ ~ ~

You will also need to provide a **SEARCH BOX (14)** and **CONTEXT-SENSITIVE HELP (17)** to make the site more usable, and provide a **SENSE OF LOCATION (15)** using **BREADCRUMBS (23)**, a **NAVIGATION BAR (25)**, the **RHETORIC OF ARRIVAL AND DEPARTURE (20)**, **STRUCTURED MENUS (19)**. A **USER-CENTERED SITE STRUCTURE (13)** will provide a far better experience.

Contributors and sources

Paul Dyson.
Dave Sissons.
Veen (2001).

景 13   User-centered site structure ★

AKA   **TASK-CENTERED SITE STRUCTURE**

*Predict what concerns
your users might have.
NHS Direct Online
screenshot produced by
the Department of
Health.*

You are constructing a **SITE MAP (12)** and trying to decide how best to organize it. Pretty much the only thing you've got to go on is what you found out using **ESTABLISH THE USE CASES (3)** and **CLASSIFY YOUR SITE (11)**.

~ ~ ~

Problem   Sites concerned with modeling, problem exploration, and so on are best built around key business objects but some workflows have to be enforced.

The UK's NHS (National Health Service) Direct site shown opposite appears to be organized around what its designers think are frequently asked questions. The dominant use case here is a request for information on a medical topic of real or imagined concern to a member of the public.

Navigation schemes should correspond to the way people think about the domain, not the way the vendor sees it. As an example, consider a user, like the present author, who decided some years ago to learn to play the Irish tenor banjo and needed tutorial material, music and possibly a teacher who lived locally. Searching the web using Netscape produced the results shown in Figure 3.7.

You are here: Home > Netscape Search > Search Results

Search Results for ' irish banjo '

Reviewed Web Sites   1 - 3 of 3
Web sites reviewed and categorized by a team of editors.

- Worried Lads, The
  Santa Barbara, CA band plays pop favorites from the 13th through 21st centuries using guitars, banjo, accordion and five-part harmonies. Irish folk, Tex-Mex and Caribbean tunes all contribute.
  http://www.worriedlads.com
  found in: Arts > Music > Styles > Folk > Bands and Artists > W

- Wednesday Tunes - Old Time Fiddle Jam
  A listing of weekly jam sessions and music and dance links in the Florida region. Jam sessions support fiddle, banjo, guitar, mandolin, dulcimer, bass, and bodhran, playing Old Time southern dance tunes with a few Irish tunes thrown in now and then.
  http://members.tripod.com/beach_music/Tunes/tunes.htm
  found in: Arts > Music > Styles > Country > Old Time

- Blackbirds, The
  A modern Irish/Celtic traditional group in Minneapolis. They play music from Ireland, Scotland, Wales and Brittany on clarinet, piano accordion, whistle, banjo, bouzouki and guitar.
  http://www2.bitstream.net/~sadams/blackbirds.htm
  found in: Arts > Music > Styles > World > Celtic > Bands and Artists

Figure 3.7

In search of a banjo teacher on www.netscape.com

Nothing local, nothing about musical instruments, nothing about sheet music, nothing about tuition! Netscape have considerably changed and improved their site since this problem was encountered.

Other search engines and searches led to sites concerned with the manufacture and sale of banjos. The point here is that the designers of sites and portals make assumptions about the users' intentions. This is all very well if the guesses are accurate. However, it is usually better to try to understand use cases for a wide range of users.

Nielsen (2000) reports that at one site, usability tests showed that users succeeded in their tasks only 9% of the time when they used navigation organized according to the mental model of the site's owners. Using a navigation scheme based on the users' tasks as they perceived them gave a success rate of 80%. Such a 9:1 difference could easily be the difference between a commercial site's continued existence.

One way to get help with the problem of how to explore the problem structure and the users' views of it is to focus on the use cases. The goals or post-conditions of the use cases need a vocabulary that supplies the 'domain ontology' i.e. the type model of the domain. Graham (2001) discusses this from a non-usability point of view but Pawson's (2002) work on expressive systems provides a particularly useful interpretation and useful guidelines.

Therefore   **Build the site structure around the use cases, especially if it is a workflow site. Establish the users' domain ontology and build the site around the business objects, especially if it is a problem exploration site. Adopt the philosophy of expressive systems.**

~ ~ ~

You will need to ensure that **CONTENT IS LINKED TO NAVIGATION (76)**.

Contributors   Richard Dué.
and sources   Detlef Vollmann.

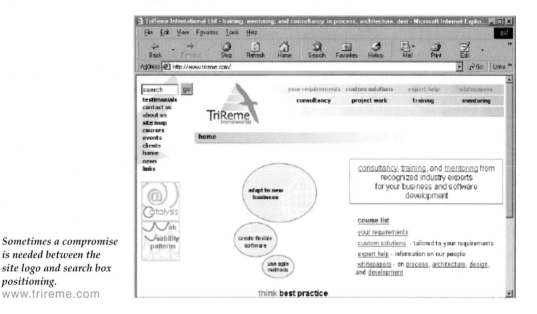 14   Search box ★★

AKA

SEARCH ENGINE

Sometimes a compromise is needed between the site logo and search box positioning.
www.trireme.com

A user may not know how to navigate to the required content based on **NAVIGATION BAR (25)** or **SITE MAP (12)**. Using it might be a slow, slow way to get there or the content may not be present – leading to waste of the user's time.

~ ~ ~

Problem

There are two ways for a user to get to required content: following predefined connections (SITE MAP) or by a content-based search. It is impossible to know in advance which will be the best way for a user to go directly to the content they need.

The paradigm for content-based or keyword search on the net is that of a user typing a string of words or phrases into a text box, followed by an Enter keystroke or a click on a search button. Because we want to let the user exploit transfer effects, it is best to support both options.

Because we **FOLLOW STANDARDS (36)**, the button should be labelled 'Search' or 'Go'; we prefer the former if space permits. Using an HTML search button is usually faster than using a graphic. Preformatting the text box with the word 'search' is another option: you don't need a button at all then. However, it means that the user has to select and delete that word before typing their query – and that's extra work.

Choosing the optimal size for the text box involves balancing the amount of space it occupies with the ease of entering and editing search strings. At a minimum, do not limit the length of the string that can be entered to the size of the box: allow the user to scroll left and right to edit the string. You may be able to guess the length of a typical search string based on known use cases or on the length of phrases related to your own content. If so, this provides a first guess as to the size of the box.

Putting it at the bottom of the page is almost always a bad idea. It may then appear below the fold and never be discovered. The best place is near to the **SITE LOGO AT TOP LEFT (24)** because this is where users have come to expect to find search facilities. Place the box and button to the right of the logo or immediately below it. If this is difficult, stay close. On the TriReme site shown above, the designer first wanted it on the right: it would nearly always remain visible because he used **MAGIC MARGINS (60)**. However, nearly is not always and most users look first on the left. Because of the shape of the logo, this looked quite ugly, so in the end he wrapped the site logo around it so that it almost becomes part of the logo.

Provide help on the search string syntax. This is one of the rare cases where providing help is appropriate.

Therefore

Always provide a search engine. Put the search box at the top of every page, preferably near and to the right of the SITE LOGO AT TOP LEFT (24). There should be a button labelled Go or Search, preferably to its immediate right. Balance the size of the text box according to the considerations given above. Carriage return should duplicate the effect of Go/Search. If possible, make the search box part of the NAVIGATION BAR (25).

~ ~ ~

Invoke a general search engine from this box, but also provide **CONTEXT-DEPENDENT SEARCH CATEGORIES (63)** where your content is capable of classification.

Contributors and sources

Paul Dyson.
Dave Sissons.
Veen (2001).

戻 15   Sense of location ★★★

You are concerned with making your site as convenient and user-friendly as possible. The user needs to map their location in the content jungle that is the site. They may ask: How did I get here? How can I get back? What is nearby?

You already know how important **FEEDBACK (41)** is. Therefore you want to provide feedback on the user's location. It is important for users to relate the location in the site to the corresponding one in their mental model of it. You are building on the **SITE MAP (12)** and a **USER-CENTERED SITE STRUCTURE (13)** to provide this.

~ ~ ~

Problem

How do you indicate to users where they are and what the context is, including routing information?

There are several ways by which a visitor might reach a page within your site. All is probably well (in a well-designed site) if they have navigated from the home page. However, perhaps they got the URL from an acquaintance by e-mail, retrieved a bookmark, used a search engine or followed a link from someone else's site. You need to assure the user that they are where they think they are or tell them where they have actually ended up. The information provided by the browser is usually not noticed by users and, in any case, is probably insufficient

Having a brand logo on every page helps say, at least, what the site is – providing the logo is well-known or self-explanatory.

A **NAVIGATION BAR (25)** should provide information as to the site structure and nearby content. It should display a visual hierarchy if possible. If the user has arrived from another location in your site the **BREADCRUMBS (23)** will help too. But we defer discussion of these patterns until we get to them.

Every page should be named carefully. This clarifies the location and its function for the user. If the page name corresponds to frequently used search strings, your site will get better scores from search engines. So find out what the common searches are (rather than the strings you think people ought to search on). Services that provide this information include Word Tracker (www.wordtracker.com).

If the user navigated to the page by clicking something, then that something should have the same name as the page.

Use newspaper style headlines to display the page name. Center it above the content it refers to.

If possible, name your pages using URLs that are easily read and interpreted by humans. This too will reinforce a sense of location.

Therefore

Always make sure that you provide visitors with clear cues as to where they are on every page, however they arrived there. This gives a sense of location in the surrounding context. Several important patterns help with this as discussed below.

~ ~ ~

Use **CANONICAL LOCATION (21)**, i.e. use a **NAVIGATION BAR (25)** and **BREADCRUMBS (23)** and make sure that you have the **SITE LOGO AT TOP LEFT (24)**. Do this within a **THREE-REGION LAYOUT (26)**. Use microsite branding (color, logo, etc.) Use **STRUCTURED MENUS (19)** and insist upon **THE RHETORIC OF ARRIVAL AND DEPARTURE (20)**.

Contributors and sources   Chris Simons.

昊 16   Aesthetics ★

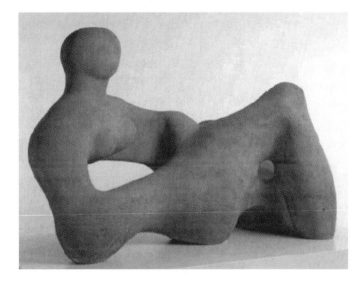

Recumbent Figure 1938.
Reprinted by kind permission of The Henry Moore Foundation and the Tate Gallery, © Tate London 2002.

You are designing the site and have developed a **SITE MAP (12)** and all the elements of the basic site structure. You want the site to be useful, usable, fast and sticky but also to look really good.

~ ~ ~

Problem

How does one now balance good graphic design with performance and usability? Appearance makes a lot of difference to a site but pretty graphics can impede usability and performance.

It is remarkable that the most liked features of a given GUI are often the aesthetic ones. One of the most popular innovations in windows systems, for example, was the 3D push button that appears to depress when clicked or held clicked. It apparently contributes nothing, but it is loved by users to the extent of being a prerequisite for all such systems nowadays.

Many sites are developed by teams that include specialist graphic designers and marketing experts. These people often dominate the design process to the extent that the sites end up looking really pretty but their pages take far too long to download. The **KISS (38)** pattern is completely ignored.

Therefore

Learn design principles such as few colors, golden section, perspective, etc. **TESSELLATE GRAPHICS (54)**. Use graphics to reinforce the function of screen areas. Use **NATURAL METAPHORS (56)**. Display **CONTENT BEFORE GRAPHICS (55)**. Use **WORDS BEFORE ICONS (57)**. Don't let any one group within the team dominate the overall design.

~ ~ ~

You will also need to understand the **USE OF COLOR (53)**. **ACCEPTABLE WORDING (50)** is also part of the aesthetics of your site.

圀 **17**   Context-sensitive help ★

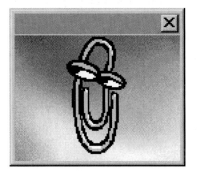

*Microsoft Office's
context-sensitive help:
Office Assitant*

You have **ESTABLISHED THE USE CASES (3).**

~ ~ ~

Problem

The utility of help messages depends on the context in which they occur and, in particular, on the task or workflow that the user is engaged in.

This is such a well-known and general pattern that it is hardly worth elaborating further. However, two things must be said.

First, if you are having to provide help at all, it may be that you would be better employed in making the feature of the site concerned more intuitive and more in line with the users' mental models and previous experiences.

Second, you cannot establish the context fully unless you understand the use cases completely. This is especially true for workflow sites where users are carrying out transactions. The context then includes the stage of the transaction reached, whether commitments have been incurred, security status, whether the transaction has failed at any point so far, and what kind of user is this likely to be. Perhaps failure was a result of a line failure or site outage. Provide feedback on this if possible. You should also inform the user of alternative paths through the transaction (if any) – maybe they went down the wrong route in the first place. Rather than helping them complete the transaction, it may be better to advise going back to the start in such a case, but always explain why you are offering the advice being given.

This pattern is related to Tidwell's **OPTIONAL DETAIL ON DEMAND**.

By the way, how many paperclips *does* it take to change a light bulb?

Example

It is extremely common to be told that you have filled in a form incorrectly. Many sites still don't tell you why. A message like 'parsing error' is no use to man nor beast. You might even tailor you 404 message (see 404.com for some amusing examples).

Therefore   **Make help messages dependent on context and workflow step, if any. Display the use case as part of the help.**

~ ~ ~

Use **ACCEPTABLE WORDING (50)** when creating help messages as well as when writing content.

Contributors   Richard Dué.
and sources   Detlef Vollmann.

3.3   Enhancing usability

This section introduces some patterns that have a direct influence on usability. They help to make the site easier to navigate and add to its interest, leading to a stickier site if applied well. For the first time, we see some completely abstract patterns that introduce basic psychological principles and their application to usability – starting straight away with the abstract pattern 18.

As in the last section, the patterns are organized according to a graph as shown in Figure 3.8, and they are numbered and color-coded. This diagram is used on the *wu* website as a means of navigating among the patterns. Clicking on a pattern name will take you to its description. Clicking on cross-references (pattern names) in the body of the pattern description also links to the pattern clicked upon.

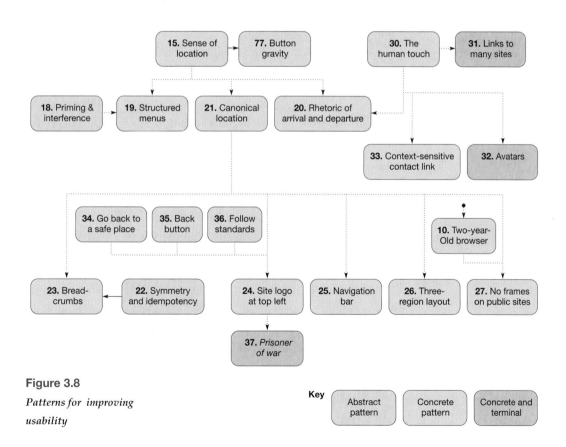

Figure 3.8

Patterns for improving

usability

Key

昴 18   Priming and interference
[Abstract] ★★

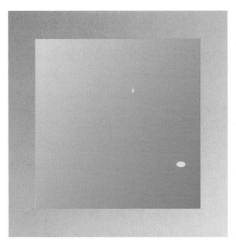

*Abstraction is the basis
of all consciousness*

Problem

Good designs should take account of the cognitive abilities of human users. How can we exploit what is known about human memory to improve our designs?

According to current theories of cognitive psychology, long-term memory (LTM) stores knowledge and data. To be used, these memories must be activated and this takes time. They are normally stored in an inactivated state, although not necessarily in a separate location from those immediately accessible in what used to be called short-term memory. Working or activated memory is limited and transitory. Items in working memory can be accessed directly and quickly. The activation of the linkages to these memories decays over time. Miller (1956) discovered that activated memory could hold a maximum of between five and nine items or *chunks* before filling up in some sense. These limits depend on the meaning of the material, and an expert's chunk can represent far more knowledge than that of a novice. It is a crude mistake to interpret this as meaning, for example, that there should never be more than 7±2 items presented on a screen. For example, when a novice sees a display of a chess board, he sees 32 pieces. A grand master, however, may see only five high-level game patterns, which she has chunked through long practice. Further, the units are stored in classification, composition and other structures that assist recall. **Rehearsal** of cues helps storage in LTM and retrieval, through reinforcing commonly used activation paths in the brain's neural network. Another way of activating these paths more quickly is **priming**, where recalling one item helps to activate another semantically related one. Priming helps activate concepts in working memory (WM). When a user moves from one system's interface to that of another, there are **transfer effects** due to both rehearsal and priming. These transfer effects can be both positive (beneficial) and negative (harmful) from the point of view of usability. The more that user interface designers are aware of memory characteristics, the better they can do their job.

Other memory effects that may be significant include **interference**, which occurs when priming may activate the wrong things or at least activate memories that interfere with what should be recalled. This is an example of a negative transfer effect. Positive transfer effects can exploit the ability of users to classify their knowledge, and this helps with the consistency and coherence of an interface. Generally speaking, positive effects will occur when the designer copies the structure of existing and well-known tasks. The success of the desktop metaphor can be regarded as evidence for this proposition, as can the popularity of tricks such as 3D button controls that appear to depress as they are clicked. A classic example of negative effects was the use of the F3 key for the help function in WordPerfect when most packages use F1. When a WordPerfect user presses F1, the wrong things are primed, and when trying to recall what key gives help there is no such support. An example of the exploitation of positive transfer effects is the support for Lotus syntax in Excel.

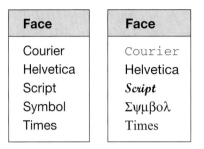

Figure 3.9

Priming memory of typefaces

Priming effects occur between semantically related words. For example, saying 'cat' primes 'dog'; showing *italic* may prime **bold**. Another example of the beneficial exploitation of priming effects in a user interface occurs when the actual appearance of an item is used to reinforce the memory of what selecting that item may imply, often using a visual cue or an icon. Fgure 3.9 illustrates this with an example of two different menu designs for the typeface selection within a word processor. The right-most menu clearly helps the user remember what typefaces like Courier and Times Roman look like. However, this can go too far. A user unfamiliar with the Greek alphabet might well be very confused by the Hellenic appearance of the Symbol face. Priming is a context-sensitive effect and designers should understand this. For example, 'cat' could prime 'X-ray' rather than 'dog' in the context of medical diagnosis.

Ensure that you understand these phenomena. Whenever possible, take account of priming and interference effects when you design the site. Most visitors will not have the opportunity for rehearsal, so exploit transfer effects where possible. Use widely understood metaphors.

~ ~ ~

Use **STRUCTURED MENUS (19)**. **FOLLOW STANDARDS (36)** to exploit rehearsal and transfer effects and avoid interference effects. Prime the user using **THE RHETORIC OF ARRIVAL AND DEPARTURE (20)**.

器 19   Structured menus

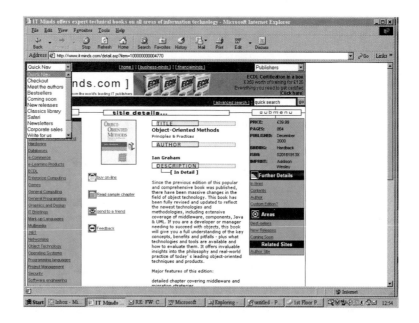

You have developed a **SITE MAP (12)** and a **NAVIGATION BAR (25)**. You realize that you want to put more information in the navigation bar than will fit easily on to a normal-sized screen and you want to avoid the need for the user to scroll horizontally. You want users to be able to **CHOOSE FROM A SMALL SET** (Tidwell) but again there are more categories than you would like. You understand the concepts of **PRIMING AND INTERFERENCE (18)**.

~ ~ ~

Problem

Pull-down menus will save space in this situation. However, they need to be given small set structure. Furthermore, users have to be able to realize that they are there.

As we know from pattern 18, structure and organization help priming. This can be seen readily in Figure 3.10. In (a) related items are adjacent and the lines emphasize this. In (b) there is no such organization and the menu is confusing to read and difficult to remember.

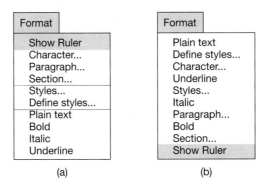

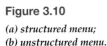

Figure 3.10

(a) structured menu;
(b) unstructured menu.

HTML provides no way to do this – and no control over things like fonts, format and spacing. Putting lines in therefore wastes space but is worth trying if the lists are not long.

Similar considerations apply when using pull-down list boxes (combo boxes). With very long lists, such as lists of place names, they are often the only solution. If you do use menus, there should be some cues to indicate that they are there.

The IT-minds site shown above makes effective use of pull-down menus to save screen space in the navigation. An old version of *The Times* site used rather long ones and, as they were unstructured, they were hard to take in at a glance. These pull-down menus had items that appeared below the fold and if you tried to scroll down the menu would disappear – and you couldn't pull them down until you scrolled up again; catch 22! That assumed you even knew that what you couldn't see was there. Resizing the window was the only solution. Admittedly, we used quite a small window but the principle stands that designers need to think about such issues carefully. In an even earlier version of the site, some menus were obscured by text boxes. The design should avoid the possibility of users covering up content with menus. We noted incidentally that the service navigation bar disappeared stage right; indicating, perhaps, that the **MAGIC MARGINS (60)** pattern had also not been applied – because of the fixed length of the menu bar.

www.trireme.com approaches the same menu problem by pulling out the menus horizontally instead of vertically. However, some users reported being confused at first by this strategy, probably because it was unusual at the time.

Therefore

Save space in the navigation by using short and, if possible, structured menus. Consider pulling out the menus horizontally if they are not too long and providing your usability and get-it tests indicate no problems are so caused. Ensure that there is a visual cue to tell the user that the menus are there.

~ ~ ~

This pattern is terminal within this language.

昊 20   The rhetoric of arrival and departure ★★★

Getting the message across

You are concerned with providing the user with a **SENSE OF LOCATION (15)**.

~ ~ ~

Problem

Link information should be visible on the current page but too much of it would take up too much space.

This pattern comes directly from Nielsen (2000). Always provide information about where the user came from when they arrive somewhere and explain why they should leave and what to expect at the destination.

Links should define content before departure to a new page. Therefore, link names should be chosen so that they make sense in terms of what they link to. Reinforce them with pop-up link titles that appear when one rolls over the link (tool tips) – the overhead for this is quite small. Warn the user if there are likely to be surprises, e.g. log-in needed or site often down. If possible, explain what benefit a user will obtain by following the link.

Changing the pointer shape for outbound links provides reinforcement but may confuse casual users: they know what the hand does, but what's this funny-looking thing?

On arrival, the page name and header should match the link title – so that the user gets **NO UNPLEASANT SURPRISES (46)**. Provide visitors with a clear **SENSE OF LOCATION (15)**.

Lastly, when you update the site, avoid potential visitor disappointment by *never* changing page names. Divert visitors to new pages if necessary.

Therefore

Use pop-ups to show at least link titles and possibly more explanation of where the link leads to. Consider displaying the URL too – especially if the user leaves the site or the site area. Consider changing the pointer shape for outbound links. Each page should contain a visible explanation or clue as to what it is consistent with the link text and title. Use BREADCRUMBS (23) to reinforce this strategy. Don't delete page names from your site – divert instead.

~ ~ ~

Make sure that you **TRACK MULTIPLE IDENTICAL REQUESTS (61)**.

Contributors and sources

Nielsen (2000).

21   Canonical location ★

YOU ARE HERE

You are trying to give users a **SENSE OF LOCATION (15)**. Search engines are a commonly used entrance route into your site. They parachute users into a landscape from a **SEARCH BOX (14)** to a location that you cannot predict.

~ ~ ~

Problem

How do users know where they are in the site? How do they get back to the site without using the search engine again?

There are several ways to reinforce the user's sense of location. The first is to let them see where they are clearly with a prominent name for the page and an indication of its location relative to the site map. The page title can be used as a headline for the main content of the page. Try to use sensible and meaningful names for the page URLs as well. If possible, use the title for the URL segment. This will help users to locate pages in future and help search engines to locate and classify your content.

Refer to **SITE LOGO AT TOP LEFT (24)**, **NAVIGATION BAR (25)** and **BREADCRUMBS (23)** to see the different ways of telling users where they are. The first tells them whose website they are on, regardless of how they got there. The second tells them their location relative to the broad structure of the site. Breadcrumbs shows them the location in terms of a single path from the home page.

Therefore

Make sure the page name is displayed prominently and above the fold. Build 'cross-links' across the site hierarchy. Use **BREADCRUMBS (23)** and a **NAVIGATION BAR (25)**. Put the **SITE LOGO AT TOP LEFT (24)** on every page. Find a way to help the user record or bookmark the site and page addresses in the history.

~ ~ ~

Since they may interfere with navigation, there should be **NO FRAMES ON PUBLIC SITES (27)**. Allow users to **GO BACK TO A SAFE PLACE (34)**.

Contributors and sources

Chris Simons.
Gareth Sylvester-Bradley.

晃 22   Symmetry and idempotence
[Abstract]

Problem

A user performs two actions in sequence that he regards as opposites but does not get back to exactly the original state or location. He may become confused and disoriented. Doing the reverse of something should get you back to where you started from. In geometry, this is called symmetry. There are other operations that, if repeated, should not change the state at all. These are called idempotent operations.

~ ~ ~

Symmetrical action is related to patterns such as **BACK BUTTON (35)** and **GO BACK TO A SAFE PLACE (34)**. If you go back and then forward, you should return to the same page. However, what back and forward mean to the user may not correspond to the way the browser sees things. For example, if you have been through several screens to complete a purchase, then going back can either be viewed as reeling back through these screens or as returning to the screen you were looking at before you hit the purchase button. Good sites include a 'continue shopping' button that has this effect.

Some operations should have no effect when reiterated. For example, when the escape key returns to the main menus hitting it twice should have no further effect. When deleting files, one should not be able to re-press the delete key to delete the next file without some other interaction intervening. The cut, copy and paste actions should also be idempotent. Idempotence is particularly important when the type-ahead buffer is active, since unintentional actions might otherwise be performed when the machine cannot keep pace with typing.

Example

With an accelerating mouse of the sort found on many Unix systems, try moving three inches to the right quickly and then three inches to the left slowly. The pointer will not end up where it started. If you were not looking at the screen, you could assume that it did – and then perform the wrong action. One soon gets used to this, but for someone who also uses a symmetric mouse regularly the situation is impossible.

Therefore

Always make sure that all user actions are symmetric, and idempotent unless you can make a strong justification for not doing so. Include this principle into USABILITY TESTING (7). Make sure that the 'back' concept is related to the use cases and include 'continue shopping' links where appropriate.

~ ~ ~

With this in mind, think about including **BREADCRUMBS (23)** in your site.

Contributors and sources

This pattern is adapted from Thimbleby (1990).

23   Breadcrumbs ★★

Jakob Nielsen's site
www.useit.com

You are trying to provide users with a **SENSE OF LOCATION (15)** and, in particular, a clear **CANONICAL LOCATION (21)**.

~ ~ ~

Problem

How can users see where they are relative to the site's home page, which probably offers more navigation options than other pages?

The site shown above uses breadcrumbs and a search box as its sole navigation. This works well for a site consisting mostly of articles and reviews, and the site is well worth a visit if you are interested in usability. Breadcrumbs provide a depth-oriented navigation bar. They show you how the current page is related to the home page.

Don't use them in place of a well-chosen page name.

Therefore

Do not rely solely on breadcrumbs for navigation unless you are very short of space. Breadcrumbs should be complemented by a NAVIGATION BAR (25) and/or other navigational devices. Some navigation, however, may be available only from the home page, but breadcrumbs need to go on every page.

Put breadcrumbs near the navigation bar and always at the top of the page. Make it clear that they are a secondary form of navigation, perhaps by using a lighter or smaller font. Highlight or embolden the current location. Separate them with a > symbol or other pointer-like device. Clarify their function by saying 'you are here'.

~ ~ ~

Next, **DISPLAY THE OPTIONS (79)** and use **NAVIGATION BAR (25)** in parallel with this pattern. Put the **SITE LOGO AT TOP LEFT (24)**.

Contributors and sources

Krug (2000).
Nielsen (2000).

旲 24   Site logo at top left ★★

www.it-minds.com

You have developed a **SITE MAP (12)** but users visit sites other than yours. Channel switching between different site layouts causes cognitive dissonance and extra work. Therefore you **FOLLOW STANDARDS (36)**. Users need to know that they can always **GO BACK TO A SAFE PLACE (34)** and may not be able to rely on the **BACK BUTTON (35)** to do this. A prominent logo will also support a user's **SENSE OF LOCATION (15)**.

~ ~ ~

Problem

How do I know which site I am currently on? How do I know what will happen when I click on the site logo? How can I always get back to the site's home page?

Since most sites place their logos at the top left of every page and use them as links to their home pages, users come to expect this. It is guaranteed to be visible when a page loads, and even when a user arrives from a search engine they will know whose site they are on. Therefore follow the standard. The logo on the home page can be larger than on other pages and may have a tag line. The tag line needs to be chosen carefully because it must differentiate and characterize your enterprise without naming it. Among the best ones we've seen, we'll mention BabyCenter who use the phrase 'cradle and all', which seems to sum up what they sell very well. The trouble is that thinking up such a phrase is very difficult.

Therefore

Follow the standard. Place your logo at the top left of every page. Clicking on the logo always takes you home. No time is spent looking around for the home button. Spend time thinking up a good tag line.

~　~　~

Fit the logo into the **NAVIGATION BAR (25)**, within the home page's **THREE-REGION LAYOUT (26)**. Avoid making the user a *PRISONER OF WAR* **(37)**.

圀 25   Navigation bar ★★

www.amazon.de
and
www.amazon.co.uk

You have created a **SITE MAP (12)** and want to make it accessible to the user.

~ ~ ~

Problem

How can the number of clicks the user needs to make to get from one section (or major section) of the site to another be reduced? How can we ensure that the user knows their location relative to the site and relative to the web as a whole?

A navigation bar lists either the top-level structure of the site or the use cases it offers. Many sites list the high-level services down the left-hand side and the use cases across the top.

Highlight the current location in the navigation bar by changing its color, emboldening it or using an image or character that looks clearly like a pointer. Preferably do at least two of these things.

Reinforce the idea that your navigation bars are to do with navigation by using a unique color background for navigation throughout the site.

Items that should go on the bar for all sites include:

◆ the site logo (which takes you home consistently);

◆ information about the organization or company;

◆ privacy policy;

◆ contact information.

For workflow or sales sites, you should include:

◆ registration and log-in;

◆ checkout;

◆ shopping basket;

◆ account information.

Other possibilities include:

◆ downloadable items;

◆ site map;

◆ communities;

◆ frequently asked questions;

◆ news and press releases;

◆ jobs.

Structural links, which point to other parts of the site, should be displayed consistently on each page to reinforce user understanding of the navigation scheme. However, this takes up a lot of space and sometimes a compromise solution is needed. The service navigation bar, usually displayed left, shows the breadth of the site but occupies a lot of valuable screen space. Therefore, consider placing it only on the home page – only a click away via the site logo, which *is* on every page.

Index card tabs are a commonly used metaphor on navigation bars, with Amazon sites being the best-known example, as shown in Figure 3.11. Notice how color is used to connect the current navigation options to the current tab. This works a lot better when there a only a few options. As Amazon's product range has been extended, the usability of the sites seems to have degraded slightly. Also, at a glance the All Products combo box on the German site doesn't seem to do anything but duplicate the tabs – or does it restrict the search somehow? Here is something that could well confuse users – and confusing people is bad. Amazon supplement this navigation with a vertical bar

SEARCH

Books

or use Books Power Search

BROWSE

Browse Categories
A-Z: Fiction
Art, Architecture &
Photography
Audio Books
Biography--New!
Business, Finance & Law
Children's Books
Comics & Graphic Novels
Computers & Internet
Crime, Thrillers &
Mystery
e-Books--New!
Fiction
Food & Drink
Gay & Lesbian
Health, Family &
Lifestyle
History--New!
Home & Garden
Horror
Humour
Mind, Body & Spirit
Music, Stage & Screen
Poetry, Drama &
Criticism

Figure 3.11

www.amazon.co.uk

on the left that contains deeper navigation options. Notice how the different placement of the combo box makes its function much clearer.

Browsers change the link colors for sites that have already been visited. This is helpful information and should not be overridden or hidden in any way. Nielsen's studies indicated that the standard link colors should be retained to maximize usability.

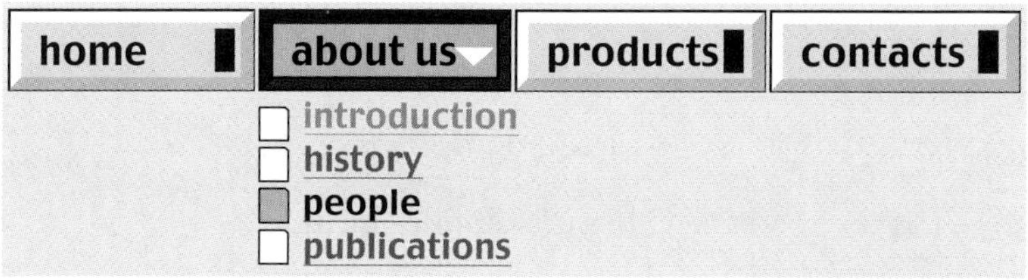

Figure 3.12

Show users clearly their current location and where they've been already.

As in Figure 3.12, use color to indicate the current location and where the user has been already. Try to **FOLLOW STANDARDS (36)**, then anything clickable will be underlined.

Avoid using pull-down menus for navigation. The user has to perform an extra action to see what the options are, and the links don't change color when visited in these lists.

Therefore

Provide a bar on the home page – and possibly on other pages – that allows the user to jump to any section of the site or at least the top three levels. Place it above the fold. Consider the use of the tab metaphor if there are less than about seven categories.

~ ~ ~

Next, include **BREADCRUMBS (23)** and make sure that the are **NO FRAMES ON PUBLIC SITES (27)**. Embed the navigation bar in a **THREE-REGION LAYOUT (26)**. For large sites, consider using **STRUC-TURED MENUS (19)**.

Contributors and sources

Paul Dyson.
Dave Sissons.
Krug (2000).
Nielsen (2000).
Veen (2001).

图 26 Three-region layout ★★

AKA

GRID LAYOUT; TILED WORKING SURFACES (Tidwell); **REPEATED FRAMEWORK** (Tidwell)

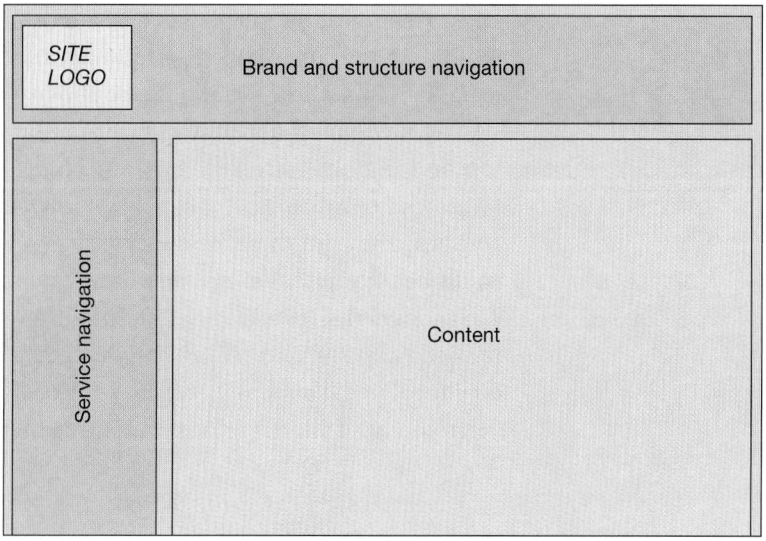

You have attempted to **CLASSIFY YOUR SITE (11)**. You are aware of the need to **FOLLOW STANDARDS (36)** and exploit **PRIMING AND INTERFERENCE (18)**. You have a **SITE MAP (12)**. You have positioned the **SITE LOGO AT TOP LEFT (24)** and begun to think about the **NAVIGATION BAR (25)**.

~ ~ ~

Problem

How can a user, arriving at your site's home page, or any other of its pages, determine where they are in the site, what content is available, and what other pages there are to visit?

The layout of a magazine or newspaper tells its reader quickly where key information is and where to start reading about it.

Headlines stretch exactly across the articles they refer to. Sidebars highlight important content and provide indices to it. One reason that this works is that people are used to it and exploit transfer effects, as described in **PRIMING AND INTERFERENCE (18)**. Similarly, many websites are laid out in a very similar way to the picture above, so that users know quickly what to do when they arrive at a site laid out in this way.

Three-region layout is very common on websites and people will be able to recognize it and benefit from transfer effects. The usual layout is shown in the figure above.

The navigation and brand information is usually shown at the top and may include advertising. This is often the best place to locate the **SEARCH BOX (14)**. This shows the user where they are and how they got there. The service bar is usually on the left, but it could be right-justified provided that you use **MAGIC MARGINS (60)**. This shows the user where they might go next. Content occupies the central panel and will usually display the page name and various headlines. This shows the user what they have found.

If you need more regions than three then so be it – but try to do it with three first.

If you design the three (or more) regions using just one table, the browser will have to download all the HTML before it can begin to render it on screen. Making the site logo and top navigation bar (with the search box of course) into a separate table will mean that the user can get a much faster sense of location and even get on with searching the site without waiting for the page content to arrive.

Therefore

Lay out the home page and possibly other pages as a grid. Start with three basic sections: a navigation and brand section usually across the top, a service navigation bar on the left or right, and the page content. Use separate tables where possible and avoid nesting tables without good reason.

~ ~ ~

Next, make sure that you use **MAGIC MARGINS (60)**. Apply this pattern in parallel with **BREADCRUMBS (23)** and **NAVIGATION BAR (25)**. Make sure you render **CONTENT BEFORE GRAPHICS (55)**.

Contributors
and sources

Veen (2001) calls this pattern 'three-panel layout'; Cato (2001) refers to it as 'grid layout' which is more general, implying, as it does, more than three areas.

吴 27   No frames on public sites ★

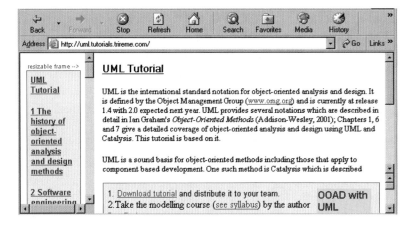

You are building a dynamic site. In this context, one needs to keep track of how changes in one part affect others. Frames are useful for viewing multiple things on one page. It is tempting to use a frame to display the **NAVIGATION BAR (25)** permanently. Some sites (e.g. letsbuyit.com) try to help users to stay linked to them using a frame. This is good for business but not always what the user wants.

~ ~ ~

Problem

You have to display multiple things on the same screen. You know that a TWO-YEAR-OLD BROWSER (10) may not be able to cope with frames and the appearance of your site on them will be messy and unpredictable. There are also problems with sizing, such as when using new bars at various resolutions. Quite often, using the back button may cause multiple copies of a frame to be displayed, looking messy and reducing the space available for content. Using frames also makes printing a mess. One can get trapped in a frameset when linking to another site. Frames can interfere with the back button and with bookmarks.

This is a typical design trade-off. Expending a little more effort to use something other than a frame will slow the project down but, for a public site, will make the site more usable for more people.

If you do include a frame, and the justification is sound, then if it is resizable, say so. For the page pictured above (on trireme.com), the justification is twofold: TriReme's customers are mostly in high-tech industries and therefore likely to have modern browsers; also, the use of frames to index tutorials is something of a standard.

Therefore

Don't use frames unless you have to and the site is an internal one. Use layers and tables instead.

When there is multiple content, cut and paste it to multiple pages. Where this content is dynamic, automate the pastes.

If frames are essential, then make sure that all links have a TARGET="_top" attribute in their anchor tag (e.g. <A HREF=xxxx.htm TARGET="_top">), i.e. replace all frames with a new frameset so that bookmarks and other navigation work properly. Always try to develop a site version that doesn't use frames or include a <NOFRAMES> section in the code.

If you must use frames, then make sure the server supports HTTP keep-alive.

~ ~ ~

You will also need to use **SEPARATE PRINT PAGES (47)**.

Contributors and sources

Andy Harbach.
Jari Worsley.
Nielsen (2000).

旲 28   Home page ★

AKA   **FRONT PAGE, SPLASH SCREEN**

Alexander Gordon
——— and Co ———

Estate Agents, Surveyors and Valuers
Members of the National Association of Estate Agents

| For Sale | To Let | Search | Mail List | Contact |

Alexander Gordon & Co., members of the National Association of Estate Agents, are based to the north of Hyde Park at Lancaster Gate and Specialise in the sale and letting of all types of property in the Bayswater, Marble Arch and Lancaster Gate areas of Central London.

Friendly personal service combined with many years of local experience ensures that Alexander Gordon & Co. are able to offer Buyers, Sellers, Landlords and Tenants a full, comprehensive and professional service

www. alexander-gordon.co.uk

You are starting out on the site design and want to get the value proposition of your organization over to the user clearly. You may also want to use the home page to explicate the site structure via a **SITE MAP (12)**. You have used a **NAVIGATION BAR (25)** and **BREAD-CRUMBS (23)** with a **THREE-REGION LAYOUT (26)** to make it obvious how to get to any piece of content on the site. You have included a **SEARCH BOX (14)**. You now have to finalize the design of the home page. You consider using a splash screen or devoting the home page to a similar function. However ...

~ ~ ~

Problem   **Everyone sees it; everyone owns it! The home page has to engage the interest of every visitor no matter what their interests and tastes. How can you convey your message to visitors as soon as they reach this page? They may go no further if you cannot do this.**

Splash screens may be helpful for first-time visitors, helping to orient them in relation to the site's content and structure. But regular and repeat visitors will be incensed at having to download this unneeded material before they can get on with the job in hand. How can you offer a splash screen only to people who need or want it?

The home page should state clearly and succinctly what the company or organization does. It needs to tell the user:

◆ what is on the site;

◆ how to navigate around the site;

◆ what they are likely to enjoy on the site;

◆ what has changed since their last visit;

◆ what benefits they will gain from a visit.

Be sure to include a search facility unless your budget is very limited. Place the search button to the right of the search text box or underneath it. The word 'search' is preferable to 'go', but it occupies more space, so there is a trade-off. Avoid putting your search engine on a separate page (except for advanced searches).

Put shortcuts to frequently used or important pages on the home page. Ensure that the logo takes you back to home from anywhere in the site.

You may have to display a registration form if you are charging customers to visit your content. However, an 'Enter Site' home page is very annoying. Sites with 'adult' content have some justification for warning accidental visitors that they may find the material distasteful, but we cannot think of many applications where such a page can be justified except when the site is multi-lingual and visitors have to select a language before proceeding. Even in these cases you might offer a registered user the chance to skip the splash screen in the future.

You may have to reserve space for advertising. Try using animated rectangles to cycle the adverts and attract attention. This saves valuable space on the page. Put news or promotions (or clear, explanatory links to them) on the home page.

Be honest: if you're tracking users' clicks, then tell them so.

Include 'last updated' information and maybe make it a link to the webmaster's contact details. Always include 'about us' information or a link to it on the home page.

Use clear, unambiguous terminology that most visitors will understand.

Nielsen and Tahir (2002) critique 50 home pages and are well worth consulting for ideas. They also give 113 specific guidelines for home page design.

Van Duyne's **UPFRONT VALUE PROPOSITION** and **HOMEPAGE PORTAL** cover some of the same issues as this pattern.

Therefore

Pay more attention to the design of the home page than any other. Make the logo larger on the home page than on other pages within the site. Try to think up a tag line that captures the essence of the site and display it prominently near the top of the page. Tell the user what the site is about.

Don't clutter the home page.

If you decide a splash screen is justified, use an applet with a checkbox asking: 'Display this screen every visit?' Use a cookie (or similar) or log-in to record **RETURN VISITORS (68)**.

~ ~ ~

This pattern is terminal within this language.

Contributors and sources

Gareth Sylvester-Bradley.
Nielsen and Tahir (2002).

🐓 29   Trite fonts

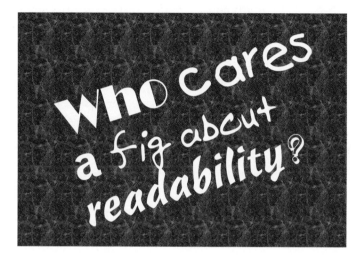

You have realized the need for as much **AUTOMATED TESTING (6)** as possible. And you respect the **KISS (38)** pattern.

~ ~ ~

Problem   **Some users will not have any fonts other than Times Roman and Helvetica (or variants of these). Using fancy fonts can give unpredictable results.**

Provide a list of alternative fonts with:

    <FONT FACE>="Palatino, Times New Roman, Times Roman, Serif">

Make sure that the fonts you use are the commonly available ones; clichés are good in web design. It is a world where most access is through PCs using Times New Roman and Arial. Offer alternatives, such as Times Roman and Helvetica for Mac or Unix users.

Therefore   Use trite fonts (and list several alternatives). Only use the
                             commonest (Times, Arial) fonts or include substitution rules in
                             your HTML (e.g. Arial becomes Helvetica) – and test them
                             thoroughly.

                                             ~ ~ ~

                             This pattern is terminal within this language.

晨 30　The human touch

THINGS FROM YOUR LIFE

www.trireme.com

You have **ESTABLISHED THE BUSINESS OBJECTIVES (1)** and **CLASSIFIED YOUR SITE (11)**.

~ ~ ~

Problem

Using computers can be an alienating experience for some. How can we make the site seems friendlier? How can we make the experience more fun?

Sites that give webmaster@daftname.com as the address for contact are not revealing much about their attitudes. Perhaps the staff turnover is high. Try to give genuine, useful personal information, as you would if someone telephoned you: 'Hi, it's Ben.' On pages that contain information on personnel, consider including a picture, but make sure it does not make **DOWNLOAD TIME (42)** too long.

Personal pages might also include information on hobbies and pastimes. Linking to related sites also makes the site more interesting and human. Ben is an a professional anthropologist but an amateur musician. He plays the button accordion (or melodeon). People who are interested in this fact (rather than his expertise in the traditions of the Kwara'ae people) might want to know where they can buy a melodeon or where they can listen to melodeons being played. So why not link to a music shop site or a list of pub sessions where such instruments can be played?

There are limits to this. Abbey National improved their site by removing the lifestyle section, which was rarely visited. The point is that it was not related to the reason people visited – looking for mortgages – and there were other sites that did the job better.

A good example of a site with the human touch is the BBC Radio 3 children's site. There are games, including a fantastic musical composition game. You select instruments (marimba, piano, etc.) and rhythms, and slot your selection into a bar structure. Kids of all ages can learn by experimentation how the different combinations sound and can write quite sophisticated compositions, with a little practice. It is important to note that all the games are educational in some way and are thus related to Radio 3's mission as a cultural ambassador.

Therefore

Include personal and 'fun' content. Link to interesting content on other sites (e.g. sites about your hobbies and pastimes) but make sure it is relevant to the central theme of the site. Contact pages should have names and pictures. Jokes are allowed, but again they must be pertinent. Above all, avoid nasty aphorisms like 'Enjoy!' or 'Thank you for shopping with ...'.

~ ~ ~

Consider providing a guide to the site using an **AVATAR (32)**. Provide help and enhance personalization with a **CONTEXT-SENSITIVE CONTACT LINK (33)**. When you link to other sites, **USE THE RHETORIC OF ARRIVAL AND DEPARTURE (20)** and avoid making the user a *PRISONER OF WAR (37)*.

Contributors and sources

Richard Dué.
Detlef Vollmann.

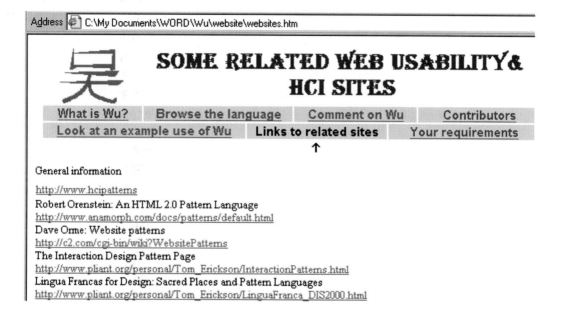

吴 31   Links to many sites

You want the user to be able to return from linked sites and to add **THE HUMAN TOUCH (30)**. You also want your site to be listed by as many search engines as possible and to be near the top of the lists.

~ ~ ~

Problem

How do you make your site more useful and interesting? How do you get search engines to notice your site and rank it highly against common queries?

Search engines use multiple criteria to rank websites against common queries. One criterion is the number of links out to other sites. But beware if you link to sites that do not exist: some engines will not list you or will downgrade your relevance ranking. Also, sites that you linked to successfully may disappear or relocate.

Therefore

Always include many links to other sites that may interest potential users. Avoid linking to sites that disable the BACK BUTTON
(35). Test the site thoroughly for broken links. Repeat the tests at
every update, in case linked sites have changed.

~ ~ ~

We need to interest the visitor and make them want to be a **RETURN
VISITOR (68)**.

昊 32   Avatar

The Kwara'ae people
live in central Malaita,
an island in the Solomon Islands.
A good introduction is
Kwa'ioloa and Burt (1997).

*Avatar reproduced
courtesy of*
www.curiouslabs.com

You are trying to add **THE HUMAN TOUCH (30)**.

~ ~ ~

Problem

Users get lost and confused. What is the best way to provide help and guide them round the site?

The best way is to keep the site simple, but when this is not possible and you need to impress users with your technical sophistication (provided that the business objectives so dictate) or highly complex content, then consider converting the help system into an animated guide using sound or animations.

An avatar should not only move and lip-synch but also contain a mental model of the user's current knowledge and task. Artificial intelligence techniques are required for this. However, this isn't as difficult as it sound since there are several rule engines available as Java components.

Microsoft's Intellisense™ wizards are simple examples of avatars, but much more is possible and software to help with the task is also available. For example, Curious Labs' Avatar Lab™ enables the creation of articulated, bendable, 3D characters for use in exploring Adobe Atmosphere™ worlds. It contains libraries of pre-made heads, hands, torsos, legs, feet, hair and props. With this software you can create custom avatars, bring them to life, and use them to explore and communicate with others in online worlds. Your web avatar can even have your own face from a front and side photograph. The avatar can be rotated and viewed from any aspect. A free trial can be downloaded from http://www.curiouslabs.com/products/avatarlab/index.html where the above image was taken from.

Therefore

If the cost of doing so justifies it, create a friendly guide. If a key business objective is to project a high-tech image and/or be ultra-friendly, or if the content of the site is very complex, then use artificial intelligence techniques and consider an animated talking head.

~ ~ ~

This pattern is terminal within this language.

Contributors and sources

The concept of avatars on the web originated in science fiction (Stephenson, 1992) a few years before companies like British Telecomm built the first prototypes.

䍃 33   Context-sensitive contact link

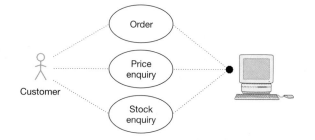

You want to provide **THE HUMAN TOUCH (30)** and use **THE RHETO-RIC OF ARRIVAL AND DEPARTURE (20)**.

~ ~ ~

Problem

The problem is to direct the user to the contact that can help with the problem being solved. Is this a query about an order or a product specification?

In order to direct the user to the contact who can be most helpful, we need to know what the user is doing. The simplest way to obtain this knowledge is to ask, but even then we need to interpret the answer. The soundest way to do this is to base our reasoning on the known use cases (pattern 3).

Therefore

Create a set of forms or menus that ask the user about the problem they are trying to solve. Associate reasoning about the suitability of the contacts you will suggest to the use cases.

~ ~ ~

This pattern is terminal within this language.

Contributors and sources

Richard Dué.
Detlef Vollmann.

昃 34   Go back to a safe place

You are concerned with providing **CANONICAL LOCATION (21)**.

~ ~ ~

Problem

The problem is once more to stop users getting lost or disoriented.

This is already a pattern in Jennifer Tidwell's language so we only touch on it briefly here. At a minimum, users should be able to go back one step using the **BACK BUTTON (35)** or a built-in facility to unwind a transaction. Bookmarks may be used, but many users find this to be merely additional workload.

Therefore

Provide a way to allow users to mark places they wish to return to if they get lost. Ensure that transactions can be unwound safely.

~ ~ ~

Place the **SITE LOGO AT TOP LEFT (24)** so that users can always get back to the home page. **CACHE TRANSACTIONS (67)**.

35   Back button ★★

AKA

GO BACK ONE STEP (Tidwell)

You understand the need for users to be able to **GO BACK TO A SAFE PLACE (34)**.

~ ~ ~

Problem

People make mistakes. Especially on a workflow site, the user should always be able to return to the previous step, undoing any commitments they may have made.

Consider arrival at the home page of a site and clicking on the *About Us* link. Clicking on the **SITE LOGO AT TOP LEFT (24)** takes one to the home page (as it should). Clicking the back button at this point will take the user forward to the *About Us* page. This will confuse the user because the browser sees a straight line of interaction and the users and designers probably think of the site as a network or hierarchy.

For example, the *wu* icon on this page (on the *wu* website) takes you back to the diagram but you can also use the browser back button.

Therefore

Do not disable the browser back button. Design transactions so that they are undoable. Provide built-in checkpoints in transactions that users can return to.

~ ~ ~

Ensure that there are **NO MODES (40)**. **DISPLAY THE OPTIONS (79)**. There should be **NO FRAMES ON PUBLIC SITES (27)**. Employ **THE RHETORIC OF ARRIVAL AND DEPARTURE (20)**.

**Contributors
and sources**

Richard Dué.
Jennifer Tidwell.
Detlef Vollmann.

 36 Follow standards

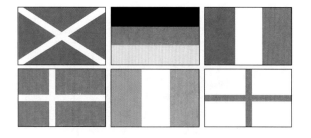

You understand the effects of **PRIMING AND INTERFERENCE (18)**.

~ ~ ~

Problem

Standards inhibit creativity but help usability due to transfer effects.

Users bring knowledge of interface and web conventions when they visit your site. If you don't follow them, you may confuse people. At the very least, you're making them think harder. The best thing to do if you want to offer something new is to consider extending a convention rather than replacing it with an entirely new approach. For an example of this, see the discussion of **SITE LOGO AT TOP LEFT (24)**. There must be a measurable benefit for you and your users whenever you deviate from a standard.

If your site has internal conventions, stick to them rigidly on pain of confusing and alienating users.

Some standards that we take for granted in other GUIs, such as scrollbars, are less effective on websites. Make sure the standards that you follow are appropriate in the context of the web.

Shopping trolleys are now a standard for commerce sites.

Therefore

Apply *de facto* and *de jure* standards. Consult style guides.

~ ~ ~

Use **ACCEPTABLE WORDING (50)**.

📧 37   *Prisoner of war*

'Get me out of here'.
Image reproduced
courtesy of Dorland
Kindersley/Guy Ryecart

You want users to have a **SENSE OF LOCATION (15)** so you have put your **SITE LOGO AT TOP LEFT (24)**. However, you sometimes need to take them from your site to someone else's.

~ ~ ~

Problem

How do you ensure that users know where they are and can get back to your site?

This is the first antipattern in *wu*. Many websites have a horrible habit of having their web pages open additional browser windows without being asked (often without the usual window paraphernalia (scrollbars, close-boxes, etc.), thus making it difficult for the average web user to close them). This is especially common with portals. The user may or may not be able to get back using the back button, depending on the site they arrive at. You have no control over this.

Furthermore, frame-based pages sometimes open additional framesets inside themselves ad infinitum – making it very hard to escape from.

Therefore

Use **THE RHETORIC OF ARRIVAL AND DEPARTURE (20)** to tell users that they are visiting a site outside yours. If you open a new browser window, offset it a little so that the original window is still visible and, if possible, your site logo can still be seen. Where possible, avoid linking to sites that disable the back button.

Avoid nested framesets; or if this is impossible, provide a link so that users can **GO BACK TO A SAFE PLACE (34)**.

~ ~ ~

This antipattern is terminal within this language.

Contributors and sources   Gareth Sylvester-Bradley.

3.4   Adding detail

This section introduces some more abstract patterns and patterns that provide more detail on how to make the site more usable and friendly and how to make it look better (Figure 3.13).

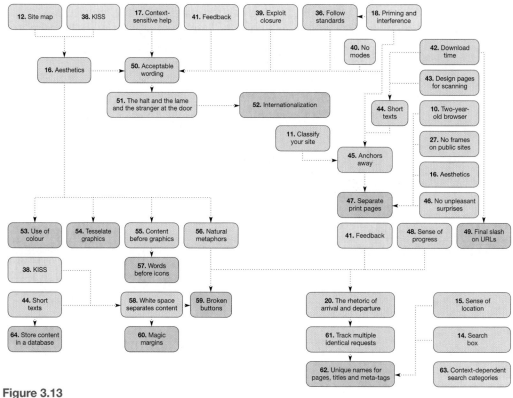

Figure 3.13

Patterns for adding detail to a design to enhance usability even further

🀫 38   KISS *[Abstract]*

    KEEP IT SIMPLE ...

Problem   **Simplicity is one of the key aspects of good design, but some domains are inherently complex.**

This pattern is the core principle that underpins all of Jakob Nielsen's writing on the web. It is a very simple principle to state. Albert Einstein put it like this: things should be as simple as possible, but no simpler.

Simplicity is enhanced for the user when business objects are exposed directly, as argued by Pawson (2002) in his work on expressive systems.

Therefore   **Remove everything from the design that is not central to the message you wish to convey. This includes images and content that are not the reason that people come to the site. Expose business objects in the design.**

~ ~ ~

AESTHETICS (16) nearly always benefit from simplicity. Try to ensure that **WHITE SPACE SEPARATES CONTENT (58)**.

昆 39   Exploit closure *[Abstract]*

Problem

How do you ensure that users complete a set of related tasks or transactions?

An important principle of user interface design that derives from an understanding of psychology is exploiting **closure**. We are all familiar with the 'I came in here for something but can't remember what' syndrome. It occurs because of the human tendency to be satisfied with tasks once we have achieved closure in one respect; we tend to omit completing ancillary tasks. This is why most bank ATMs make you take your card before taking the money. The alternative sequence is likely to cause errors because once you have the cash (closure of main task), you are likely to depart, forgetting the card and receipt. Unfortunately for the street sweepers, the same principle is rarely applied to the receipt as well.

Therefore

When designing workflows for your site, decide what is the main task and force the user to complete necessary subsidiary tasks first. Provide FEEDBACK (41) as the various tasks are completed.

~ ~ ~

Next, consider **ACCEPTABLE WORDING (50)** in the way you give these instructions and confirmations.

圆 40   No modes *[Abstract]*

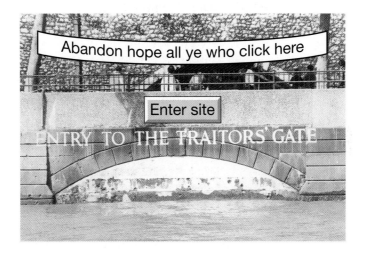

Problem

How do you give the user a sense of being in control of their own destiny when using your site?

Modes in a user interface are defined as 'variable information in the computer system affecting the meaning of what the user sees and does'. In a **modal** system, the user is required to know what mode the system is in because the same action may have quite different effects in different modes.

It is commonly agreed that modes should be avoided but that they are sometimes necessary. For example, having *user* and *novice* modes is agreed widely to be almost a principle in its own right. Certainly, the system should inform the user of the current mode and it is good practice to attract attention to the change by a change of color in the mode indicator, a status bar or some such device. Examples of modes in an interface include: pressing the on button on a typical calculator, where the mode is either *on* or *off* and the effect is different in each case; a 'Cannot save file – disk not formatted' message reveals a mode; as does 'Overwrite existing file?'. Dialog boxes are usually modal in that the behavior of other visible options is suspended while they appear; the behavior of part of the screen has thus changed. The notion of modes is related closely to that of polymorphism; polymorphic interfaces are precisely modal. However, what is useful in a language is not necessarily good in an interface.

It is very helpful to provide users with information about the context within which their actions will be interpreted. This includes information on state dependencies and modes and should explain the current task with its pre-conditions, post-conditions and side effects. Modes should be used only where it is absolutely necessary to restrict the user's freedom of interaction. Temporal modes can be used to enforce a certain sequence of operations but this implies burdening the user with a heavy load on memory. This should never be done useless out-of-sequence actions are catastrophic. The commonest example of this is the excessive use of cascaded modal dialog boxes where a simple data entry form would do better. Spatial modes are common when several things are possible but only one can be done at a time. Highlighting icons and changing the mouse pointer are good ways to draw attention to spatial modes. Other contextual information can be given in a status bar, such as the state of the irritatingly-close-to-the-main-keyboard 'insert' key on most PCs.

It is generally wise to include *undo* and *redo* facilities to encourage exploratory learning and protect users from catastrophic errors. However, *undo* and modelessness can be incompatible as Thimbleby (1990) demonstrates, though the argument is too intricate to summarize here. It is largely because undoing multiple actions may change the state of the system in other ways. Modern interfaces often respond 'can't undo' when they encounter this situation.

Thimbleby gives the following principles for modes, breaking them down into principles for pre-emptive, inertial, input and output modes, along with a general principle of equal opportunity:

◆ *Pre-emptive modes*. You should be able to do anything anywhere (e.g. there should be no Y/N questions or immovable dialog boxes).

◆ *Inertial modes*. The layout of successive screens should change as little as possible. When you go back, everything should be as you left it. The most [recently | likely | frequently] used menu selection should be highlighted.

◆ *Input modes*. The system should be sufficiently consistent to use with the display switched off (e.g. q or Alt-F-X for quit).

◆ *Output modes*. WYSIWYG.

The last of these of course is inapplicable to web design. The first is a pattern in its own right.

One of the commonest examples of modality on the web is a disabled back button. Another, where there is no option but to switch modes, is the 'confirm purchase' button.

Therefore

Try to avoid modes when you design the site, especially when implementing workflows. Use modes only when you need to stop the user causing damage or when transactions are necessarily irreversible. Warn users before switching modes.

~ ~ ~

Consider **EQUAL OPPORTUNITY (65)** and **AVOID PRE-EMPTION (66)**.

昆 41   Feedback *[Abstract]*

Problem   **How do you make sure the user knows what the results of their mouse clicks are?**

The simplest feedback device is perhaps the electrical thermostat. Such a device measures the output temperature of a device such as an iron and switches off the current when the temperature reaches a predetermined, but possibly variable, value. Should the temperature fall below that value again, as it usually will, the device can turn the switch on again. Biology is replete with examples of benefits from feedback devices: from the balancing of a jellyfish based on feedback from its very small nervous system to the accurate footfalls of an Olympic hurdler based on a complex tableau of feedback from visual, tactile and possibly other sense organs.

The principle of feedback is central to user interface design. When it is not provided, users make mistakes. If they make mistakes they will not return to your site.

Examples

When selecting an HTML button over a graphic button, we must consider that the former will be faster and will render in a familiar way on various operating systems so that users can exploit transfer effects. Perhaps the most important reason for using proper 'buttony' buttons is the feedback they provide by appearing to be depressed when clicked (at least on PCs).

Another common example of lack of feedback occurs when the user clicks on a link and nothing appears to happen for a while. This can be disorienting and can lead to errors if they keep on clicking. Progress bars built into most browsers are not always prominent enough to attract the user's attention and sometimes are misleading.

Therefore

Every time you design a feature of the site, think how it will provide information to the user. Ask whether the user will be able to predict the effect of every action they can take. Will they always know what the new state is? Use progress indicators in addition to those provided by the browser.

~ ~ ~

Give the user a **SENSE OF PROGRESS (48)**. Employ **THE RHETORIC OF ARRIVAL AND DEPARTURE (20)**. Avoid **BROKEN BUTTONS (59)**.

昊 42   Download time

You know that performance and users' impatience, lack of free time, work pressure and perceived cost of communications will affect users' attitudes to your site. Since you have **ESTABLISHED THE USE CASES (3)**, you can deduce the kind of download experiences they are likely to have. Since you have adopted **AUTOMATED TESTING (6)**, you want to test and collect metrics on download and display times. Everyone wants a sticky site.

~ ~ ~

Problem

Users leave if download times are not short, especially on dial-up lines. Users who leave a site in dismay will usually never return. For any site, this is undesirable; for commercial sites, it is catastrophic.

The size of a file in kilobytes (don't even think about megabytes) gives some indication of the download time it will need. However, this is only approximate and is unpredictable due to variable network latency, site traffic and error correction. One of the worst sites in this respect that we have found varies from almost instantaneous download to several minutes – apparently dependent on the time of day. One deduces that testing for this is not done, rather than that the designers are so underpaid and abused that they just don't care.

One can carry out usability testing: going through the use cases with a stop watch or collecting timing data using a product such as Speed-trap's Prophet.

Perceived time is not always the same as actual time. If the user has something interesting to do or look at during a download, they may be more tolerant. The overhead of downloading an animation may pay for itself in this way, but it *must* be useful and relevant to the task.

To reduce latency caused by the need to establish a new connection for each object, make sure that the server supports HTML keep-alive.

Therefore

Keep the page sizes small enough such that download times are less than ten seconds on a 28K modem using SHORT TEXTS (44). Avoid nested tables, which will slow downloads. Provide FEEDBACK (41) and a SENSE OF PROGRESS (48) using progress bars and pop-ups before download, using THE RHETORIC OF ARRIVAL AND DEPARTURE (20). Make sure that both the physical and subjective download time is tested, including on TWO-YEAR-OLD BROWSERS (10). Use AUTOMATED TESTING (6) too.

~ ~ ~

To help reduce subjective time, use **THE RHETORIC OF ARRIVAL AND DEPARTURE (20)**. **DESIGN PAGES FOR SCANNING (43)** and use only **SHORT TEXTS (44)**. Print **CONTENT BEFORE GRAPHICS (55)**.

Contributors and sources

Mattias Larsson.
Veen (2001) contains a interesting chapter on speed.

43   Design pages for scanning

> ## Welcome to *wu* news
>
> [   ] search
>
> ## Usability is trebled and productivity is doubled by using a good pattern language.
>
> Studies at **MadCap Corporation** in **Transylvania** have shown that it is possible to gain huge benefits, year on year, through the intelligent application of patterns. Speaking at InfoVamp 2002, **Vlad T. Impaler**, marketing manager for Madcap, said on Tuesday: "In our bloody and turbulent business productivity is everthing and usability is even more important than that and life

You know the importance of **DOWNLOAD TIME (42)** and appreciate that users are often busy, impatient people.

~ ~ ~

Problem

Reading web pages is an essentially nonlinear activity. But texts are inherently linear. How do we resolve this conflict?

Most people visiting sites do not read the content: they merely scan quickly, looking for relevant information or links. Headlines and subheadings help by providing **CANONICAL LOCATION (21)** and giving clues to maximize scanning efficiency.

Remember that newspaper-style headlines (like 'Gotcha!') may confuse rather than inform. Use color and bold for highlighting important text. Don't underline it, to avoid confusion with links. Write the conclusion in front of the argument for it. Consider using the conclusion as the headline (as above).

Nielsen advises not starting headlines with the same word, to assist scanning. He also, however, shows a dislike of what he calls 'cute' – by which he presumably means witty – phraseology. We cannot concur with this unless the site is intended to ignore the **HUMAN TOUCH (30)**.

Finally and rather obviously – although not to all web designers it would seem – use black and white text for maximum readability whenever you want visitors to be able to scan.

Therefore

Design pages for scanning: don't arrange them linearly. No wasted white space. Use headlines. Include loads of hyperlinks. Make use of bulleted lists and side bars. Highlight key words, phrases, sentences and paragraphs.

~ ~ ~

Include **LINKS TO MANY SITES (31)**. Write **SHORT TEXTS (44)**. Organize content for **THE HALT AND THE LAME AND THE STRANGER AT THE DOOR (51)**.

Contributors and sources

Nielsen (2000).

囻 44   Short texts

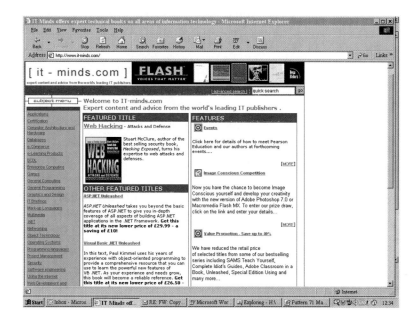

www.it-minds.com

You want people to be able to get a lot of information from your site and they want to do it quickly with minimal **DOWNLOAD TIME (42)**. You also know that people scan text on web pages rather than reading it carefully. You already therefore **DESIGN PAGES FOR SCANNING (43)**. The web is essentially a hyperlinked, multi-dimensional experience rather than a linear one as with books, magazines or music. Long, linear texts are harder to read on screens.

~ ~ ~

Problem   **The problem is to facilitate readability and maximize the rate of information transfer.**

Make the headline relevant to encourage users to read the text it captions. Try to keep the text short enough to fit in a low-resolution browser above the fold. Consider rewriting any text to make it shorter.

Then consider breaking it up into smaller chunks. A good heuristic for chunking is to ask whether a sensible headline can be devised.

This pattern is related to Tidwell's **HIGH DENSITY INFORMATION DISPLAY** and to Tufte's (1983, 1990) concept of 'chart junk'.

Therefore

Use only well-written, short texts, one per page, one per workflow step. Provide extensive links between pages. In graphics, reduce everything that does not represent data to the barest minimum.

~ ~ ~

You may now wish to take any **ANCHORS AWAY (45)** and split your document into separate, linked pages. With **SHORT TEXTS (44)**, you can now **STORE CONTENT IN A DATABASE (64)**.

Contributors and sources

Nielsen (2000).

45   Anchors away

AKA   **AVOID ANCHORS, HALLO SAILOR, ANCHORS AWEIGH**

You are designing part of a site where the content is highly interrelated or consists of a long, structured document. You discovered this when you **CLASSIFIED YOUR SITE (11)**. You already **DESIGN PAGES FOR SCANNING (43)** and use **SHORT TEXTS (44)**.

~ ~ ~

Problem   **How does one balance ease of maintenance of the content with ease of navigation and usability?**

Coherent material, such as a software development process guide, is best organized as a single page/document. This makes it easier to maintain. It also makes printing easier.

   However, jumping around within a page upsets the browser's history. Also, if an anchor is already visible, the user may see no change when they click – leading to confusion.

Designers have added internal anchors to break up and organize long documents. This assists browsing these pages but may confuse users. Some users, for example, expect links always to take them to different pages, due to **PRIMING AND INTERFERENCE (18)** effects such as rehearsal.

Example

Many commercial instantiations of the OPEN Process by Trireme's clients are delivered as a single page with anchors. The motivation is ease of maintenance. A single diagram with hot spots is used to navigate among activity/task lists for different workflows/activities. However, experience shows that maintainability is purchased at the price of usability. It might be better to make the diagram and the different task lists into separate pages.

In general, if in doubt, don't do this:

```
<HTML>
  <body>
    <a name="top"/> Go to the top <a/>
    <! – – ... – –>
    <a href="#top"/>
  </body>
</HTML>
```

Therefore

Classify each page according to whether its content is logically separable. If it is, then turn it into many smaller pages and remove all anchors from the site.

~ ~ ~

Use **SEPARATE PRINT PAGES (47)** if the user may need to print or copy some of your content. Large pages broken only by anchors make it harder to provide separate print pages.

Contributors and sources

Gareth Sylvester-Bradley.
Alan Cameron Wills.

图 46   No unpleasant surprises

You are trying to ensure the sites has **NO MODES (40)** and you want users to feel safe on your site. You want to provide plenty of **FEED-BACK (41)**.

~ ~ ~

Problem

Reliable behavior is needed by users. They should be aware of where they are in a progression of actions. They should understand the impact of each action and be sure of its outcome (both on the site and in the world).

One step forward, one step back, where am I now? Exasperated users will leave your site. We need to exhibit consistent behavior to build trust. Progress through the site should appear logical and repeatable.

Designed artefacts should be fit for their purpose. They should be natural in behavior and conform to users' expectations. There should be no unpleasant surprises, except where these are introduced deliberately as alarms. Use of the artefact should give feedback on progress of the task being undertaken. They should fit the mental and manual abilities of users. A very common example of bad interface design outside the context of computers concerns door handles as discussed in Chapter 2.

Forms can mess up predictability (see example below) for several reasons:

◆ session time-outs

◆ poor server-side code

◆ poor integration.

Example

One bank labels sequential screens with 'Stage n' but fails to indicate which stages cause irrevocable commitment to be made. You commit at Stage 3 but it doesn't tell you this until Stage 7.

The present author ordered some beta software from a Microsoft site. After filling in a form, he was presented with a 'parsing error' screen. Assuming that it didn't like the phone number beginning +44, he re-entered: with the same result. So he tried again. Two weeks later, Microsoft's fulfiller telephoned, asking: 'Do you really want three copies of this software?'!

Therefore

Use Next and Previous buttons where appropriate; *c.f.* **BUTTON GRAVITY (77).**

Ensure consistency in linked pages by:

◆ **using pop-ups;**

◆ **when opening in a new browser window, offset it slightly or display a message saying that you are opening a new window and giving instructions on how to return to the previous context. This is Tidwell's PILE OF WORKING SURFACES pattern;**

◆ **using trapped frames.**

Ensure consistency of log-ins:

◆ **to guarded pages;**

◆ **to the home page.**

Ensure consistency of navigational links, especially if they are built dynamically. Protect against double form submission. Adopt an attitude of forgiveness: the user is not to blame for errors, it's probably your design. Allow them to undo errors. Give feedback on mouse clicks – what is the outcome?

~ ~ ~

Ensure that the user gets a **SENSE OF PROGRESS (48)**. Consider using **BREADCRUMBS (23)** and **BUTTON GRAVITY (77)**. **TRACK MULTIPLE IDENTICAL REQUESTS (61)**.

Contributors and sources

Andy Harbach.
Jari Worsley.

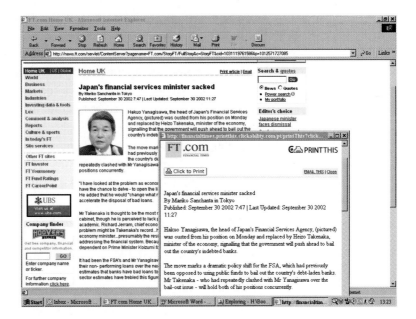

47   Separate print pages

AKA   **PERFECT PRINTING, PRINTABLE VERSION, DOWNLOADABLE CONTENT, PRINTER FRIENDLY**

www.ft.com

You want users to be able to make a record of all or part of the content of your site. Navigability and **AESTHETICS (16)** conflict with printability and other kinds of download functionality. Users want **NO UNPLEASANT SURPRISES (46)** when the data are displayed locally or the page rolls out of the printer. You cannot rely on advanced facilities within the users' browsers because they may have **TWO-YEAR-OLD BROWSERS (10)**. And you have already decided that there should be **NO FRAMES ON PUBLIC SITES (27)** so you cannot use these either. You have already broken the material up into **SHORT TEXTS (44)**.

~ ~ ~

Problem

Background images, layout, images and other content occurring over page boundaries, typeface sizing and color, page orientation, and size all cause printed material to appear a complete mess. Data formatted for easy download are not always easy on the eye either and take longer to read on screen than on paper.

Pages are usually hard to print or transfer to other applications. Printed pages often need to be taped together. The result is nearly always messy and cluttered with unwanted material.

Using applets for printing or downloading material to local drives is difficult because of the Java security model: access to printers is impeded as well as access to other devices (hard disks, etc.)

Examples

The Teaching Company Directorate (TCD) used a flash plug-in, with white text on a black background. Work was needed to reverse the colors.

Hometrack.co.uk had a long form, consisting of several (ten or more) pages, available online as ten web pages for completion offline. It was also available as a single printer-friendly web page (also ten pages long!).

An insurance company client of TriReme International allowed brokers to access their policy data via the web. Tables were extracted from a DB2/400 database and presented via an applet. Printing facilities could not be implemented.

The *Guardian* and *The Times* newspapers both offer both interactive and printable versions of their daily crossword puzzles. Interestingly, from July 2001, the latter starting charging £10 per annum for access to the printed version in an attempt to generate some revenue that was not dependent on the the contracting advertising market. This presented users with a very simple financial decision: either join the club or do the extra two minutes' work needed to create their own printable version. Regular *Times* solvers of course would probably cough up the dough. However, those of us who prefer the *Guardian* puzzle might well proceed as follows:

1 Hit the PrintScreen key.

2 Paste the result into MSPaint or similar.

3 Cut and paste the first set of clues and the grid to PowerPoint or similar.

4 Go back to the web page and scroll down to the next sets of across and down clues.

5 Repeat steps 1–4.

6 If the clues don't change, print from PowerPoint.

When you design your site, try to calculate what percentage of users will tolerate this extra effort (relatively minor in this rather bizarre case).

Keep the page area small enough to print on both A4 and letter paper sizes. Apply this rule whether printing via the default driver, Postscript or as .PDF files. The print version of the *Guardian* crossword, which you can link to from the above page, works well and quickly. However, although they manage to print the brand bar and navigation at the top of the page and still fit the grid and clues on to the same page,[4] they then insist on printing another brand bar with no apparent purpose. This wastes a whole sheet of paper: bad for the environment as well as for the user.

Lyardet and Rossi (2001) give a very similar pattern called **PRINTER FRIENDLY**.

Therefore

Use separate pages for printing or downloading a printable or downloadable version of content in a predetermined format.

If the material is purely tabular, the alternative is to pass HTML tables directly (as objects) to another local application or spreadsheet program.

~ ~ ~

This pattern is terminal within this language.

Contributors and sources

Andy Harbach.
Jari Worsley.
Nielsen (2000).

---

[4] At least on A4 paper – which is reasonable because, expats aside, most people living outside the British Isles would probably not want this particular puzzle.

48   Sense of progress

Because of the need for **FEEDBACK (41)** and **NO UNPLEASANT SUR-PRISES (46)**, we need to feed back to users the level of achievement of their goals and, indeed, ours.

~ ~ ~

Problem

In particular, web users are often unaware of:

◆ the point reached during the retrieval of an item of content – page number, download time, etc.;

◆ the stage reached in a business process;

◆ the point of commitment or rollback of a goal.

This may lead them to making errors with dire, or at least irritating, consequences. These will mean they will probably not become **RETURN VISITORS (68)**.

The interface should provide a sense of progress. Feedback is needed for this because effects can thus be related to causes and allows the user to see if the results of each step are contributing to the overall task. Slow tasks or network delays should be made visible in this way, so that the user can tell whether the system has really crashed or is just plain slow. Changing the mouse pointer to an hourglass is a helpful and often-used technique but one can still wonder whether the system has hung. Providing an estimate of the anticipated time in the form of a gauge is useful in such contexts.

Web technology presents content one page at a time, unlike a book where we can flick through the pages to gauge progress. Steps need not be linear. Any order may be appropriate.

Examples

Putting labels on pages detailing both the current step and the total number of steps, as in Figure 3.14. Using a progress bar or gauge graphic and/or hourglass cursor to indicate progress of retrieval of a page or other item.

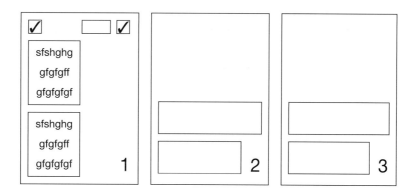

Figure 3.14
Label pages

In linear, stateless solutions, such as credit card payment for the contents of shopping basket, one may:

1 provide card number and expiry date;

2 display the total due and the payment date(s);

3 provide confirmation of payment;

4 if confirmed, commit the payment transaction and confirm its completion (perhaps by e-mail as well).

Non-linear, stative solutions, such as filling in a household insurance proposal form, one may use visual techniques such as check boxes, traffic lights (and other ways to **SUPPORT COLOR WITH SPATIAL METAPHOR (69)**) and so on.

Therefore

Make sure that a sensible indicator of commitment/rollback is displayed prominently.

Identify all the steps needed to achieve a goal and provide a visual indication of:

◆ **the current step;**

◆ **the total number of steps;**

◆ **the points at which transactions are committed.**

~ ~ ~

Consider that a transaction may, at least in the mind of the user, span more than one visit to the site. In that case, use **RETURN VISITOR (68)** and **CACHE TRANSACTIONS (67)**. Remember to **SUPPORT COLOR WITH SPATIAL METAPHOR (69)**. On workflow sites, use **PIPELINE INTERACTION (78)**.

Contributors and sources

Chris Simons.

49   Final slash on URLs

You know that users are sensitive to **DOWNLOAD TIME (42)** and that every little helps.

~ ~ ~

Problem

How can you speed up downloads from your site and from new sites that the user visits?

You should use something like http://www.daftname.com/ rather than http://www.daftname.com or www.daftname.com.
  This will fractionally decrease download time.
  Of course, most modern browsers do this automatically, but if you are constructing URLs in an applet or program of some sort, then the pattern applies.

Therefore

Always arrange to append the final slash to any URLs that the user types and correct other obvious syntactical errors.

~ ~ ~

This pattern is terminal within this language.

Contributors and sources

Nielsen (2000).

昊 50   Acceptable wording ★

www.chromatography
.co.uk

You are providing **CONTEXT-SENSITIVE HELP (17)** or textual **FEEDBACK (41)**. At the same time you want to **FOLLOW STANDARDS (36)**, **EXPLOIT CLOSURE (39)**, **PRIMING AND INTERFERENCE (18)**, and have **NO MODES (40)**. You know that **AESTHETICS (16)** must be considered.

~ ~ ~

Problem

There are ways of phrasing that are unacceptable to some users. Different wordings suit different groups. We must determine how to make the wording of instructions suit both the context and the user. Also, any dialog that the user may have with the site requires designing.

Designers should be sensitive to and understand the idiosyncrasies of possible visitors. They should not impose their predjudices on users or act like cultural imperialists. Nor should they irritate users with inappropriately chosen words.

Don't assume that users know what is obvious to you about your business processes or that they know your jargon. Many sites have failed because of this.

Examples

Not allowing a user to live in Wales (a country) or Great Britain (an island), offering only UK (which is *not* a country but a – possibly short-lived – state).

Printing APPLICATION ABORTED on a gynaecological site.

Insisting that Quakers (or anyone else for that matter) describe themselves as 'Mr' something. It's so old-fashioned.

Good dialog design requires consistency, informative feedback and simple error handling. Frequent users should be able to take shortcuts. The system should exploit and indicate the phenomenon of closure. *Undo/redo* facilities are often useful but can be problematic in cases where some actions cannot be consistently undone or redone. Dialogs should be user driven and not modal, when possible. The designer should attempt to reduce the load placed on the working memory of the user – exploiting priming, transfer effects, closure and other devices. The use of words and language itself can be important. Table 3.1 illustrates this point.

Table 3.1

Use of language in error messages

Error message	Evaluation
ABORT: error 451	Bad
I'm tremendously sorry but I have discovered that a file you want to use is already open (error number 451).	Better but far too verbose
Error number 451. File already open. This error normally occurs when you forgot to close the file at the end of a previous subroutine.	Better but tedious
Error number 451: file already open. Explain?<Y/N>:	Good-ish
Left as an exercise to the reader	Perfect

Error messages should be consistent, friendly, constructive, informative and precise and should use the users' terminology. Multiple levels of message are often helpful. Hypertext help systems are a simple way to meet most of these requirements.

Command languages should exhibit uniform abbreviation rules, be consistent and follow standards. Old counter-examples from DOS include multiple ways of abbreviating directory commands (CHDIR, CD, DIR, etc.). Also, in different operating systems from the same manufacturer, it used to be common to find several words being used for the same purpose, e.g. CATALOG/DIRECTORY or HELP/ASSIST/AID.

Therefore

Understand who the users are. Look for a universally inoffensive form of words if there is one. Then design user-specific pages if a general wording cannot be found. Always include an Other **option in drop-down lists. Design dialogs carefully based on the use cases. Use the users' terminology. And avoid jargon.**

~ ~ ~

Make sure that you have also allowed for **THE HALT AND THE LAME AND THE STRANGER AT THE DOOR (51)**. N.B. This pattern is not to be confused with the antipattern *POLITICAL CORRECTNESS*.

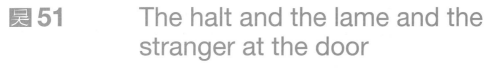 51 · The halt and the lame and the stranger at the door

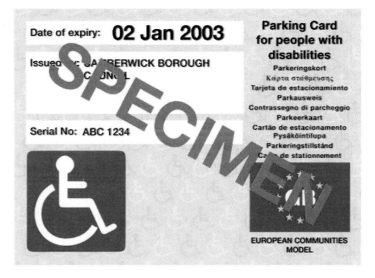

You are designing a site that will be used by people you know nothing about. You want to present them with **ACCEPTABLE WORDING (50)**.

~ ~ ~

Problem

Users may have disabilities. They might not speak your language or understand your icons. But you still want them on your site.

These days, there are legal requirements in places such as Europe and the USA to provide facilities for the disabled and one should, at a minimum, become familiar with the relevant legislation and make sure that the site complies. In Australia, the first damages under such legislation were awarded to a blind user against the Sydney organizing committee of the Olympic games.

Any site with non-textual content risks being inaccessible to the disabled. For example, text can be read aloud by the machine for deaf people but pictures cannot be interpreted other than as pictures.

Icons are often culturally specific. Thus, they should always be labelled with text in the appropriate language. Consider, for example, the misinterpretation of the two icons shown in Figure 3.15, which some us might have interpreted as 'good' and 'bad'.

Figure 3.15

Erroneous stereotyping

Moustache 1   Moustache 2

Remember that quite a few men suffer from color blindness, although it is rare in women.

Therefore

Learn the relevant legislation. Ensure your site can be read by text-to-speech programs. Be considerate. Allow for cultural difference – even encourage it. Label your icons. No red on green screens, **SUPPORT COLOR WITH SPATIAL METAPHOR (69)**, use keyboard shortcuts.

~ ~ ~

Use **WORDS BEFORE ICONS (57)** and **CONTENT BEFORE GRAPHICS (55)**. Consider your **USE OF COLOR (53)**.

This pattern conceals a great deal of complexity. We envisage the possibility of complete pattern languages for building interfaces that are usable by disabled users. If your site is intended to be accessed widely, then you should also consider its **INTERNATIONALIZATION (52)**. Advice on how to make your site more accessible to disabled users is available at www.w3.org/WAI. Nielsen (2000) provides much useful material on these topics.

昊 52   Internationalization

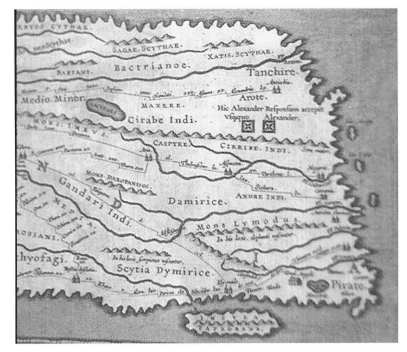

Image courtesy of Jim Siebold.

You have considered **THE HALT AND THE LAME AND THE STRANGER AT THE DOOR (51)**. This caters for users with disabilities and attitudes unknowable by you. However, your company may wish to extend into foreign markets or provide content for them. ASCII encoding militates against this. Cultures vary in more than just language.

~ ~ ~

Problem

How to make systems extensible in this context.

Example
A tourist board in partnership with a motoring organization for a German-speaking country wants to attract visitors from Yugoslavia, China, America and Great Britain. We need three new character sets.

American gallons are smaller than British ones. Even though Britain is in Europe and nominally metricated, and petrol (gasoline!) is sold in litres (liters!), car fascia computers compute fuel economy in mpg and speed limits are advertised in mph. Chinese people still think of distances in li (very approximately a mile). And so on.

Therefore

Use Unicode instead of ASCII or EBCDIC. Tag each page with the appropriate encoding. Ensure that the content databases and search engine can handle foreign characters too. Make sure that error and pop-up responses are not hard coded.

Don't forget to adjust to the local weights and measures systems, which are much more variable than you might think.

~ ~ ~

This pattern is terminal within this language. However, there is scope for a complete pattern language covering this area. Nielsen (2000) provides a good deal of discussion of the topic.

昺 53   Use of color

    USE OF COLOR (UK)

You are concerned about the site's **AESTHETICS (16)** and simplicity: **KISS (38)**.

~ ~ ~

Problem   **How do you use color effectively on a website? How do you attract the user's attention?**

There are many tricks that designers employ for getting a user's attention to focus on a particular screen location, datum or message. Galitz (1981) reported that the guidelines provided in Table 3.2 proved effective. Color is useful for gaining attention, but one should be aware that the eye is not color sensitive at the periphery. It can help in emphasizing the logical organization of a screen, facilitating subtle discrimination and improving aesthetics. Use it parsimoniously. Beware of monochrome ports; i.e. people running an application on a black and white screen that was developed on a color one and finding that certain contrasts obscure a function. This is more of a problem with printers than screens nowadays. Beware of poor contrast combinations. Allow users to change the color scheme, and above all be consistent. Another reason for avoiding thoughtless use of color is the very large number of people, especially men, who have some degree of color blindness.

Table 3.2

Gaining attention

Intensity	Up to two levels
Point size	Up to four sizes
Fonts	Up to three types
Blinking	2–4 Hz
Color	Up to five colors
Sound	Soft tones, except for emergencies
Symbols	Bullets, arrows, boxes, lines

Other guidelines for using color effectively may be stated as follows:

◆ Use color parsimoniously. Use no more than 12 colors and only five for critical tasks.

◆ Use color to increase information flow. Colors should relate semantically connected items. Color changes should nearly always be used to indicate mode changes to attract attention to them.

◆ Take advantage of color associations such as red/danger, but beware of cultural variations (e.g. white is the color of mourning in China). Use industry-standard associations where possible, e.g. the color coding of electrical wiring, or red and yellow for healthy tissue in medical applications.

◆ Allow for human limitations. The eye is usually more sensitive to yellow and green than to red or blue. The latter are therefore poor for displaying detail or small text. The luminance ratio between foreground and background should be 10:1. Embolden dark characters on light backgrounds. Use desaturated colors for backgrounds to avoid fatigue. Avoid bright colors at the display extremities to avoid flicker effects. Gray is usually best for this. Use contrasting colors to avoid problems for color-blind users.

◆ Consider the task being performed. Typeface design matters for textual presentation. Realism matters for pictures.

◆ Treat color as part of the whole interface. Be consistent. Use color as you use menu design – as a simplifier of tasks.

◆ Think about how the user will cope with motion, especially when using a mouse.

It is often effective to prototype in monochrome and introduce colors later. Further, you should not clutter display. The same technique, sound or color should indicate related items. Response times should normally be under one second. Messages should indicate significant variations. Pace-induced stress should be avoided. Novices should be allowed more time.

Tidwell's **STATUS DISPLAY** pattern is related to this pattern.

Therefore

Use as few colors as possible and reinforce semantic content with them. Use standard web colors – the priming effects will help users get to grips with your site more quickly. Remember that many men are color blind. Color blindness is rare among women.

~ ~ ~

This pattern is terminal within this language. We recommend that you consult a graphic artist at some stage during the design of any commercial site.

 # 54   Tessellate graphics

You want to minimize **DOWNLOAD TIME (42)** but still make your site look good.

~ ~ ~

Problem   The problem is to provide a flashy or attractive background that downloads quickly.

Page-sized graphics take a long time to download. However, once a small graphic has been captured by a browser, it can be reproduced many times very quickly indeed.

Therefore   Use a small graphic for backgrounds that can be repeated as a tessellation.

~ ~ ~

This pattern is terminal within this language.

昊 55   Content before graphics ★★

昊 Welcome to the *wu* website & virtual patterns w/shop

| | search |

| What is *wu* ? | Browse the language | Comment on *wu* | Contributors |

| Look at an example use of *wu* | Links to related sites |

Wu is a pattern language for designing and building usable web sites. It will ultimately be published by Addison-Wesley under the title A Pattern Language for Web Usability.
You are invited to:
– browse the patterns;
– offer comment and criticism;
– try the language out on projects;
– contribute new patterns;
– send in case studies of its use;
– send in your most hated web sites, stating howthey violate the patterns or (of course) your favourites.

download sensitizing image
[25 Kbytes]
(photo of rice paddies)

You have **CLASSIFIED YOUR SITE (11)** and you are designing pages for it. People on dial-up lines want to use features quickly, rather than wait for graphics to download; they are sensitive to **DOWNLOAD TIME (42)**.

~ ~ ~

Problem

How do you reconcile the desire for a sexy, graphical appearance with the need for lightning speed?

The simplest solution is to avoid using graphics at all, but this is rarely possible on commercial sites and never on arts and entertainment ones. However, it should always be considered because of the **KISS (38)** principle.

Paint the screen with meaningful text and obvious textual links before rendering any graphics. If you use ALT text attributes to do this, most browsers will do the right thing automatically. This is especially important (a) on the home page and (b) above the fold. Users can now follow the links they need without waiting for the graphics to load. The images can be placed quickly only if you supply HEIGHT= and WIDTH= attributes. Of course you should do this for tables too.

For especially large images, give the user the option as to whether they download them (as above). Notice that the ALT text explains both the penalty and the reward for taking the download.

It is possible to manipulate, search and process text in many other ways on current generation computers. This is not so with graphics. Text rendered as a graphic has lost its semantics. HTML and, even more so, XML go further by allowing you to add structure to text, thus adding even more meaning.

Therefore

First, try to avoid using images. Explain what each navigation option is in text before placing any graphics. Put text in the spaces where the graphics will (eventually) appear. Make the buttons clickable and use THE RHETORIC OF ARRIVAL AND DEPARTURE (20) pattern before starting the graphics download.

~ ~ ~

Now use **WORDS BEFORE ICONS (57)**.

56   Natural metaphors

You are concerned with **AESTHETICS (16)** and want to make the site more usable. You can exploit transfer effects to help with this. You understand **PRIMING AND INTERFERENCE (18)**.

~ ~ ~

Problem

What will increase the user's sense of familiarity and understanding of your site's function and features?

Metaphor and simile are powerful devices in literature and art. They work on computers too. Perhaps the most famous metaphor is that of a desktop, wherein documents are represented by icons on a plane window. The advantage of such devices is that users bring their experience with real desktops to bear on their use of the system. They know about filing documents, which helps them understand the idea of saving computer files. They know about waste paper bins, so that deleting a file can be accomplished by dragging it to the bin. This metaphor does have limitations: who keeps their waste paper bin on top of their desk? But it still works. The Apple idea of switching the machine off by dragging the system icon to the bin is an example of what goes wrong when you mix metaphors and try to extend the metaphor to a place where it doesn't work.

Authors are always told not to mix metaphors. Shakespeare got away with it, but are you a Shakespeare? Don't take it too far. The phrase 'the man is a lion' usually doesn't mean that he chases and eats zebra. Some metaphors can offend. One that offends us is the use of the words 'Colts' and 'Fillies' to designate toilets in some pubs. It's not so much that it's slightly sexist but more that it's utterly twee.

Commercial websites routinely use a metaphor based on the store guides that one sees next to the escalators in big department stores. The navigation bar will contain phrases like 'china and glass' that shoppers are familiar with. One can envisage a restaurant metaphor being useful on some sites. Imagine a bookshop site with classifications like 'appetisers', 'main courses', 'wine list' and 'desserts'. How would users interpret these categories? A possible interpretation might be that appetisers are light, newsy articles, main courses are thick novels, items on the wine list are intoxicating and perhaps erotic (or could they just be classic works), and desserts might be suitable for bedtime reading or just stodgy works about web usability. The point here is that you need to know how your metaphor will be taken. **GET-IT? (8)** tests are a possible way of finding out.

The whole concept of navigation is of course itself a metaphor. A common way in which this metaphor is violated is the use of a hierarchical list for the **SITE MAP (12)**. We think that a graph is almost always better; it's more like a navigator's chart. The idea of buttons that can be pushed is an almost universal metaphor on the web. Consistency suggests that they should look more like buttons than most of them do.

Therefore

Use metaphors that are natural to your target audience. Be consistent in your use of metaphor and don't go over the top. Consider whether the metaphor may be offensive to some users.

~ ~ ~

Use **THE RHETORIC OF ARRIVAL AND DEPARTURE (20)** to reinforce metaphor used for navigation. If your site uses the button metaphor, ensure there are no **BROKEN BUTTONS (59)**.

図 57   Words before icons

You already display **CONTENT BEFORE GRAPHICS (55)**, but now you want to include images that represent icons that are clickable. You understand the need for clarity and simplicity: **KISS (38)**.

~ ~ ~

Even when an icon or small graphic downloads quickly, it should still be supported by words. The page should be clickable as early as possible, so download the words first.

Icons are culturally specific and their use depends on background knowledge that may not be shared by all users. For example, consider the symbol shown in Figure 3.16 for a moment. You either know what it means immediately or, I suggest, will never guess. Here is a clue. Most European or American readers over 40 will have used a device with this icon in its interface. The answer is given elsewhere.

Figure 3.16
An icon

It is usually a good idea to reinforce icons with words. Download the words first.

~ ~ ~

This pattern is related to **THE HALT AND THE LAME AND THE STRANGER AT THE DOOR (51), SHORT TEXTS (44)** and **INTERNATIONALIZATION (52)**.

58   White space separates content

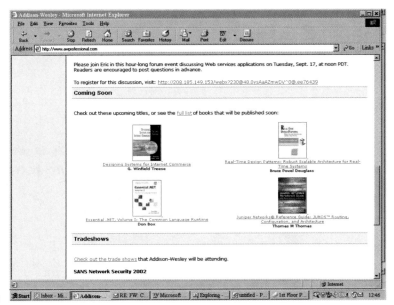

The context here is simplifying design, **AESTHETICS (16)** and **KISS (38)**.

~ ~ ~

Problem

How does one separate items of content visually without cluttering up the page and taking away its aesthetic appeal?

The general principle is that one should try removing design elements to see if the site works as well without them. Lines separating clickable text often waste valuable screen space and make automatic sizing to fit the user's screen more tricky. Horizontal lines often make people think they've reached the end of a page.

Using **SHORT TEXTS (44)** helps to enable this strategy.

Therefore

Avoid wasting space by using graphics and lines to separate content on pages that need to display different types of information. Experiment to see whether using white space to separate page areas works for your site and type of content.

~ ~ ~

Now get rid of any **BROKEN BUTTONS (59)** and use **MAGIC MARGINS (60)**.

Contributors
and sources

Nielsen (2000).

图 59   Broken buttons ★

AKA   **WRAPPED LINKS**

www.geocities.com/
wiedworks

You are including links to other pages or sites on a web page. You understand the need to provide **FEEDBACK (41)** and use **NATURAL METAPHORS (56)**. You have tried **WHITE SPACE SEPARATES CONTENT (58)**.

~ ~ ~

Problem   You don't know the size of the window a page will be displayed in. Therefore you cannot predict how your links will appear to the user.

Buttons (i.e. links) can be wrapped round to fit the window of the table cell they are in or the browser window in which they appear. People can then think that one link is two or more links. In the example below, the user could think there were four options instead of three.

Example

SCARLET **RED/AMBER** **GREEN**	COULD DISPLAY AS	**SCARLET** **RED/** **AMBER** **GREEN**

As an aside, it is also usually a bad idea to allow things like telephone numbers, e-mail addresses or people's names to break in this way.

Therefore

Avoid line breaks in links. Do not put links midstream in other text: place them on a separate line. Use non-breaking spaces.

~ ~ ~

This pattern is terminal within this language.

Contributors and sources

Spool *et al.* (1999).

昆 60   Magic margins

PROPORTIONAL MARGINS, LIQUID PAGES

www.kvetch.com

You have organized your content into **SHORT TEXTS (44)** and decided that **WHITE SPACE SEPARATES CONTENT (58)**, but your users may have **TWO-YEAR-OLD BROWSERS (10)**. You must now lay out your web pages. On the one hand, your clients want to be able to specify and control the layout down to the smallest detail. But on the other, users are using multiple browsers, browser versions, screen sizes, and screen resolutions.

~ ~ ~

Problem

How can we reconcile the competing forces that arise from the need to display rich content and to fit everything into the browser window?

The traditional approach is to use pixel-based layout, which balances these forces – but this leaves the user frustrated, by:

◆ wasted white space and less content on the screen; or

◆ cropped and/or horizontal scrolling.

It is no longer acceptable to advise visitors that they must use a particular browser or screen resolution. Instead, we must make our pages adapt to the environment in which they find themselves. To achieve this. the key is to use relative instead of absolute values for all positioning statements.

For example, we could use a table to implement part of our **THREE-REGION LAYOUT (26)** as follows:

```
<P>
<TABLE BORDER="0" WIDTH="100%">
   <TR>      <TD WIDTH="10%"></TD>
         <TD WIDTH="20%">Service navigation goes here</TD>
         <TD WIDTH="70%">Content goes here</TD>
   </TR>
</TABLE>
```

The first column represents a margin and it might be better set to a fixed small number of pixels: WIDTH="15". To see the kind of thing that can be done, consider what happens when we shrink the window display for the kvetch site shown above (Figure 3.17).

Figure 3.17

kvetch on a small screen
www.kvetch.com

Notice how the graphics that render the corners of the 3D background remain unscaled while the text in the right hand column is scaled and wrapped. The scrollbar that now appears is prominent because of its positioning and color relationship to the background. The user can be in no doubt that there is something below the line now. What a nice design! Veen (2001) gives further analysis of how this site is constructed. He also discusses the use of Cascading Style Sheets and Javascript to implement this pattern – a topic beyond the scope of this text – and allow you to have variable font sizes. The most obvious and useful application of this is to shrink or stretch headlines to fit above the content they introduce as the column width changes.

Another problem that this approach avoids is the aesthetic problem of masses of blank space appearing when the window is large. The user has to scroll to see content that could have been on the screen if the designer had worked only slightly harder (Figure 3.18).

Figure 3.18

A page designed for 600 × 480 resolution on a 1920 × 1280 display.

Therefore

Design margins that are appropriate for many window sizes, resolutions, etc. Try 5% instead of 30 pixels for margins, using tables to segregate content and other objects. Use a 1-pixel invisible graphic to enforce minimum column sizes and avoid BROKEN BUTTONS (59), also avoid using non-breaking spaces. Draw attention to scrolling that depends on window size.

~ ~ ~

This pattern is terminal within this language.

Contributors and sources

Gareth Sylvester-Bradley.
Veen (2001).

61 Track multiple identical requests

www.twinsmagazine.com

You are designing a site that requires users to complete forms or follow links. You understand the need to provide **FEEDBACK (41)** and **THE RHETORIC OF ARRIVAL AND DEPARTURE (20)**. You want to give users a **SENSE OF PROGRESS (48)**.

~ ~ ~

Problem

People need to make submissions on the web, but they can click twice on a link by mistake, because of lack of feedback or because the connection is too slow.

We are trying to make life easier for the user. One way to irritate a visitor to your site is to let them click on two apparently different links only to get to the same page. The browser changed the color of the first link, so the user knew they had been there already. Unfortunately, the same page was accessed via a different URL, so the browser couldn't know that it was the same page. The user decided not to visit the site again.

Slow connections also lead to multiple clicks. A browser back button may lead to a script being executed twice. A request is submitted several times.

Examples

1	Register for a bank account.	For an internet payment service:	
2	Get confirmation page.	**1**	Fill in submission details.
3	Hit browser or page 'back' button.	**2**	Click on submit.
		3	While waiting for a response, click submit again.
4	Be asked to 're-submit'.		
5	'Yes' leads to 'account already taken'.	**4**	Credit card is debited twice.

Therefore

Always use the same URL to refer to a particular page. Keep track of requests. Ensure that none of your pages contains duplicate information. On commercial sites, trap multiple requests either on the server side or using an applet (if they are identical).

~ ~ ~

This pattern is terminal within this language.

Contributors and sources

Andy Harbach.
Jari Worsley.
Nielsen (2000).

昗 62   Unique names for pages, titles and meta-tags

You have included a **SEARCH BOX (14)** on your site. Pages need titles and meta-tags to identify them, but on dynamic sites, if they are not updated with content, they become irrelevant. You want to be able to **TRACK MULTIPLE IDENTICAL REQUESTS (61)** and enhance the user's **SENSE OF LOCATION (15)**.

~ ~ ~

Problem

Search engines shouldn't return multiple links to same site, or they should grey out all references to a site that has been visited – even if the URLs are different. However, the browser cannot be expected to deduce that sites with different names are the same and grey them out should this be the case.

Non-unique titles and meta-tags make identifying pages difficult or impossible for searching, search engines or bookmarks. It is also important to ensure that page titles are meaningful.

If a page is referred to by two names, then a browser cannot know that both links refer to the same page. The user may well become confused or angry when they click on a blue link only to find that they have been to this place before – the other link was purple of course.

Using commonly used search keywords for page titles will ensure that search engines rate your site highly against these keywords.

Example
The search results pages of AltaVista or DejaNews.

Therefore

Use unique titles and meta-tags for static and dynamic pages. Always use the same URL to designate any given page

~ ~ ~

This pattern is terminal within this language.

Contributors
and sources

Andy Harbach.
Jari Worsley.
Nielsen (2000).

63

Context-dependent search categories ★★

You have created a **SEARCH BOX (14)** but the material on your site is capable of classification in ways that users will understand and want to exploit in their searches. You understand **STRUCTURED MENUS (19)**.

~ ~ ~

Problem

How can you support sensible classification-based searches?

On the HMV music site, it is not possible to search by record label – which is inconvenient if you are interested in an obscure genre supported by specialist labels. It is not immediately obvious whether or not one might get anything useful back by interpreting 'Artist' as 'Composer' if you were interested in the music of Sullivan, say. Sifting through a list of Gilbert O'Sullivan records probably isn't what you had in mind. Therefore, you might not bother and instead go off to Amazon, where they do things differently – not necessarily better but differently. HMV have lost a punter. Amazon has the opposite problem in that only the category search is evident when you first look at the site (see Pattern 25). It takes a while to realize that you can also do category-based searches.

So what's wrong? We think that HMV haven't thought enough about the use cases and their range of users. As a result, they haven't thought enough about the classification scheme. To be fair, the site does now allow one to search by keyword, which solves most of these problems. But this example does illustrate the risks associated with classification-based search and the need to get the classification structure right and makes sure it really covers the territory. Just for fun, see if you can add to the list of music categories listed below:

◆ artist;

◆ catalog number;

◆ composer;

◆ copyright owner;

◆ date range composed;

◆ date range performed;

◆ label;

◆ soloist;

◆ song;

◆ title;

◆ work.

Amazon need to make it clearer that there is more than one entry point to searches.

Using category-based searches addresses the need to speed up searches but is not good for finding specific, but unpredictable, content unless the category model is complete and shared by the user. A site concerning zoological types could expect this to be the case and we think that it is possible for music and book sites. For other domains, there may be no shared classification model.

Another problem with the classified search approach is that users often ignore pull-down menus or text boxes because they don't always realize that there are options other than the default that is displayed.

If space permits and there are few options, then radio buttons may be better. Place these above or below the text box to save space and indicate conceptual proximity by spatial proximity. If they are at the side, users may not chunk them with the search box.

Therefore

Prefer free text searches to classified ones unless there is a well-thought out, shared classification scheme. Include a 'free text' option among the other categories. Back up classified searches with full text searches. Make it visually clear if there are multiple places on the page from where a search may be initiated.

Make sure that there are visual cues indicating the presence of classification menus. Use radio buttons if there a few choices. Place these above or below the text box

~ ~ ~

Ensure that **CONTENT IS LINKED TO NAVIGATION (76)**.

Contributors and sources

Veen (2001).

寘 64　Store content in a database

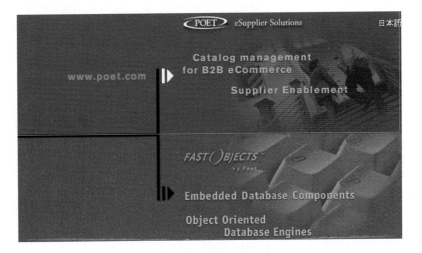

www.poet.com

You are using **SHORT TEXTS (44)** to populate your site. You know that users will be annoyed unless they get **NO UNPLEASANT SURPRISES (46)**. But your site is large and there is a need to update content frequently.

~ ~ ~

Problem

The problem is to maintain the site without having to cut and paste changes to hundreds of pages and make sure that changes to content do not interfere with the site's structure.

This pattern is a borderline case in terms of its relevance to usability. It does affect the usability from the point of view of the people who have to maintain the site of course, but it may just prevent the sort of unpleasant surprises that can arise for users when a change is not applied consistently across all pages. Therefore we include it in the language – just – but describe it only briefly.

The simple solution is to construct pages from elements that can be edited once and then included on the pages where they are needed. This can range from things like price lists that are probably stored in a database anyway right through to page headers and textual content and on to the navigation and search engine areas.

Most web servers these days support server side includes. This feature enables you to type the HTML for, say, the brand bar into a separate file called something like branding.inc and replace it in the page code with a statement such as:

<!–#include virtual="/includes/branding.inc"–>

The server can now construct the page before transmitting it to a browser. The overhead should be well worth it.

Returning to actual content, one may divide it into short texts and images and store each fragment (HTML and all) in a database. To allow access to these data, create an index page that pulls the data that describe the content out of the database itself *via* Active Server Pages or similar. This allows you to embed SQL queries in your code.

If you are running your site at an ISP, be aware that not all ISPs permit this feature; check whether yours does.

Databases do not assign meaning to the data they store. This means that a specific group of users cannot be targeted. Content-management systems add a layer of semantics to a database, usually using XML, so that documents and sections of documents can be assigned meaning. In this way, the data can be restructured for different users (personalization) or for different devices such as WAP phones. Content management systems are usually based on object-oriented database technology, which can provide better performance than relational systems in some cases, typically when the data have complex structures.

Large commercial sites and web services will almost always benefit from a content management system.

Therefore

Put every separate page element that might possibly change into a database and construct pages dynamically using server side includes. For larger, commercial sites use a content-management system.

~ ~ ~

This pattern is terminal within this language, but obviously there is a lot more to learn about databases and content management in this context.

3.5   Dealing with workflow and security

This section completes the pattern language with patterns that reapply the principles in the context of workflow sites. A few other generally applicable usability patterns are introduced too (Figure 3.19).

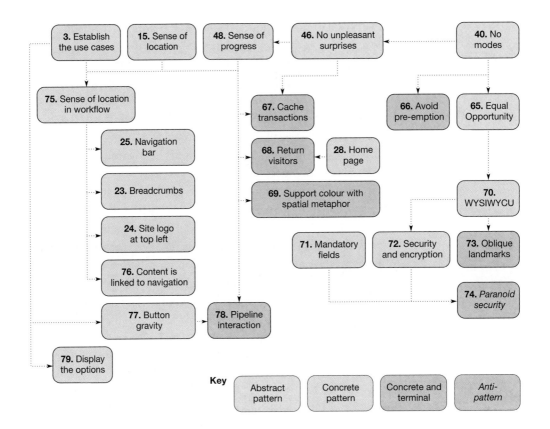

Figure 3.19

Patterns for dealing with workflow and security issues: the fourth and last group of patterns in the language

晃 65   Equal opportunity *[Abstract]*

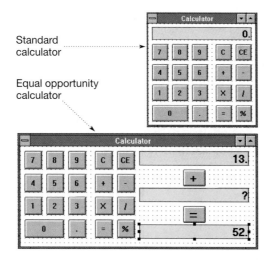

Standard
calculator

Equal opportunity
calculator

Problem

**How do you make users feel they control the tasks they are
trying to perform?**

Equal opportunity means that output can become input and vice
versa, e.g. aperture or shutter priority cameras.

Thimbleby (1990) gives the example of calculators of the sorts
illustrated above. Standard calculators are not equal opportunity
because the result and the operands are not interchangeable. For
example, I can put in '13 * 4 =' and will (with luck and a good bat-
tery) get '52'; but I cannot put in '? * 4 = 52' and expect the unknown
to be computed as '13'. Incidentally, these devices also have poor
feedback in the interface. If you want to check that 0 * 0 = 0, you may
equally well believe that the device is not working as that the algebra
is vindicated. The improved design is based on equal opportunity;
set the symbols for the two button displays, put in any two numbers,
and the third will display a consistent result. We could improve the
design further by not using 0 as the default display.

Another, better-known example of equal opportunity is Query
By Example (QBE), a widely used query method for relational and

pseudo-relational databases. QBE offers the user a blank form such as the one shown in Figure 3.20. The user may then type fixed values for Dept and Salary and QBE will return all records that match the pattern. This is not dissimilar in principle from what occurs with Prolog queries, which are resolved by pattern matching too. The equal opportunity arises because the user may choose **any** value to fix and is not constrained to a fixed, pre-designed dialog, such as:

Enter Dept: *Sales*
Enter Salary: *>10,000*
<list of matching records>

Figure 3.20

Query By Example in database enquiry systems

Name	Dept	Salary
?	Sales	>10,000

Cut-and-paste facilities usually give equal opportunity, or at least they should do.

Therefore

Try to design interactions that users may perform on your site to give them equal opportunity in the selection of the order or entry of parameters.

~ ~ ~

Equal opportunity is related closely to **NO MODES (40)**.

66   Avoid pre-emption

You are trying to ensure that there are **NO MODES (40)**.

~ ~ ~

Problem

The specific problem is pre-emptive modes. You should be able to do anything anywhere (e.g. there should be no Y/N questions or immovable dialog boxes), but sometimes there is no choice but to restrict the user for their own safety (or yours).

Modes are bad because they restrict the user's sense of being in control. Pre-emptive modes are no exception and should be avoided. However, there are situations where the user needs to be protected from rash and damaging actions for which an undo facility cannot be provided or is not guaranteed to work – when there is a crash, for example.

Non-pre-emption is a good principle because it restricts the flexibility of the interface and the range of tasks to which it can be applied. On the other hand, there is sometimes a real need for pre-emption to prevent catastrophic, inadvertent errors. The user might erase several pages by accident, delete or overwrite files unintentionally, forget to save some important work, lock the keyboard or system inadvertently, or fill memory and abort the session by accident. Such dangerous moves are candidates for pre-emptive prompts.

Therefore   Avoid pre-emption where possible, but balance the principle with
                     one of safety first. Allow forms to be completed in any order.

                                        ~ ~ ~

                     This pattern is terminal within this language.

67   Cache transactions

You have designed a workflow site and know that users may want to **GO BACK TO A SAFE PLACE (34)**. You want users to experience a **SENSE OF PROGRESS (48)**.

~ ~ ~

Problem

The problem is to capture transactions accurately. But what if a user's line goes down or their machine crashes halfway through a complex transaction?

They will be intensely annoyed if they have spent a long time filling a shopping trolley using the search engine only to revisit the site or re-establish the connection to find it empty.

In another scenario, the user may decide, halfway through a purchase, to visit another site – perhaps to check whether your prices are competitive. They will be annoyed if they return and all the details they have painstakingly typed have been thrown away or their shopping basket has been emptied.

Therefore

Cache every transaction on workflow sites. Treat registration as transactional. Cache any details entered by a user registering. Use cookies or registration to identify users returning after an interrupted transaction whether because of a crash or a decision to visit a site outside yours.

~ ~ ~

This pattern is terminal within this language.

昊 68   Return visitors

Users need a **SENSE OF PROGRESS (48)** and this extends beyond the timespan of a single visit. You may have put a splash panel on your **HOME PAGE (28)**.

~ ~ ~

Problem

How do you know whether a user has visited your site before so that you can treat them as a return visitor?

First-time visitors may need different information or treatment from returning visitors. If you have a splash panel saying what your company does, then returning users will find it annoying. They already know what you do: that's why they're back.

If your site involves registration, then there is no problem, but if not, then this is a very tricky issue, because people have different attitudes to how much the site should be allowed to know about them. New European legislation proposes that you must ask users' permission before you deliver cookies to their machines. We suggest that this is a good idea and should be done anyway. It gives the user a sense that you respect their privacy. Another problem with cookies is that they identify the machine rather than the user. A user can use two (or more) machines and a machine can be shared by several users.

If a visitor comes back often, you could congratulate them on it in some way. But this could equally well delight or upset them.

Therefore   **Use cookies to identify non-registered return visitors. Treat them differently to improve their experience. Think carefully about how they will react to being observed. Warn them before sending cookies, Javascript, etc.**

~ ~ ~

This pattern is terminal within this language.

69   Support color with spatial metaphor

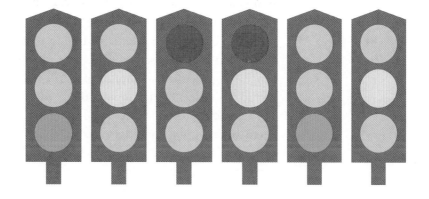

You predict that **THE HALT AND THE LAME (51)** may visit your site and you understand the need to display **WORDS BEFORE ICONS (57)** and use **NATURAL METAPHORS (56)**.

~ ~ ~

Problem

How can you ensure that colors that you have attached meaning to will be interpreted in the way you intended?

Perhaps the user is color blind. Perhaps (though it's unlikely) they have a monochrome display. Perhaps you chose stylized hand gestures. Beware that an outstretched palm is an offensive gesture to a Greek and the number of fingers you need to put up for offense varies between Europe and the USA. Perhaps red, or a chequered flag, would support the ideas of starting, or finishing, a task. If sound is an available option, perhaps a closing door noise is useful.

Even if you support your icons with words, the visual image will reinforce their meaning and get it over to the user more quickly. Also, sometime the words are covered by a graphic that downloads into the same hotspot after them. The image should carry meaning that distinguishes the colors in some spatial way.

Example

One application we encountered needed to show how recently its data had been updated. The designers decided that data that were fresh (less than five minutes old) would be shown in green and data older than two hours would be shown in red. Data with an age between these values would be shown in yellow. In this case, they were exploiting a common convention that red stands for danger and green for its absence. However, the presence of the middle range suggested the metaphor of traffic lights. This gave them the chance to reinforce the signals they wanted to send to the users with a widely understand visual image and, incidentally, insert a finer distinction (red and amber) if it were needed in the future. This would work well in monochrome in countries where traffic signal were standardized as 'red is at the top'. In this case, the users were all in Britain or perhaps the USA so the image would work. In fact, it became a much-praised feature of the system.

Therefore   **Use spatial images to reinforce and disambiguate color codes that you want to display. Ensure that the images and metaphors will resonate with the intended users, and remember that images can mean different things in different cultures and contexts.**

~ ~ ~

This pattern is terminal within this language.

昊 70　　WYSIWYCU

AKA　　　　　**WHAT YOU SEE IS WHAT YOU CAN USE**

You are designing interactive features of your site and understand
**PRIMING AND INTERFERENCE (18), THE RHETORIC OF ARRIVAL AND
DEPARTURE (20)** and **EQUAL OPPORTUNITY(65).**

~ ~ ~

Problem　　　　　How do you draw attention to features of your site?

The WYSIWYG principle is well known to GUI designers. The
acronym stands for 'what you see is what you get' and implies the
principle that all forms of output should be the same, e.g. the
layout, font and size of characters that appear on a screen will be
exactly what a printer produces. Current browser technology
makes this almost impossible to achieve on the web. The designer
cannot control how a user's browser will display content.
However, there is another principle that can be applied.

WYSIWYCU stands for 'what you see is what you can use'. If there is an object on the screen, you should be able do something to it or with it, and what that something is should be as natural and obvious as possible. Future computer systems may, I hope, generalize this to WYKAIWYCU ('what you know about is what you can use'). You know about cut and paste. Why can't you use it in a typical modal dialog box? Well, you can actually – if you know about the keyboard shortcuts, but you may have to find out the hard way.

One thing that disorients users is the appearance of things that appear to be clickable turning out not to be, violating WYSIWYCU. People tend to give up on such sites quickly.

Therefore   **Make sure that it is always clear how to use or manipulate anything that is visible on the screen. Buttons should look clickable. Menus should look pull-down-able. And if it looks clickable, it should do something (useful).**

~ ~ ~

This pattern is supported by using **OBLIQUE LANDMARKS (73)**.

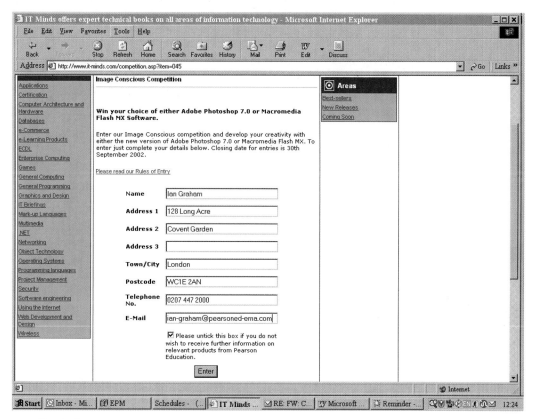71 Mandatory fields

www.it-minds.com

You know that you should avoid pre-emption in interface design. But you need to capture some information about users, perhaps as part of a workflow application. **INTERNATIONALIZATION (52)** dictates that you will often not know how users normally express themselves or describe themselves. You can predict that many of them will be impatient. You are aware of the need for **ACCEPTABLE WORDING (50)**.

~ ~ ~

Problem

The problem is to capture the essential information without trying the patience of the user or upsetting their sensibilities.

Many websites offend in this respect. It is a common experience to fill in a form only to find that the site rejects the input because:

◆ fields have been left blank; or

◆ entries have not passed the site's validation.

Many users will give up and go elsewhere rather than re-enter their particulars.

    If you are validating text, explain the rules so that the user has a chance of getting it right first time. For example, explain that there are to be no hyphens in telephone numbers, if this is what you want.

    Tidwell's **FORM** pattern is related to this pattern.

Therefore

Make the absolute minimum number of fields mandatory. Give the user an Other **option wherever possible. Always indicate visually which fields are mandatory. Use a star to do this and change the background color of the mandatory fields. Explain any validation rules to the user before they do any typing. In case of validation errors, present the form again.**

~ ~ ~

Avoid *PARANOID SECURITY* **(74)** checks.

 72   Security and encryption

You understand **WYSIWYCU (70)** but do not want the wrong users using the wrong things.

~ ~ ~

Problem

The problem is that of security. User must only be able to do the things that the law or your policy permit. Sensitive data must be protected and often encrypted when in transit.

Security is not a usability issue, but the way it is presented is. Use secure, verifiable sites for transactions that require security. Tell the user when they enter and leave these areas, but do not frighten them unecessarily with messages about the dangers of the internet.

If you can see a feature, you want to be able to use it. Being locked out can be annoying. This means that you should avoid displaying things that are not usable. If security really means that some users will be locked out of features, then tell them why – and make sure it's a good reason.

Cookies are a useful way to make visiting sites that require registration a more user-friendly experience. However, some users are wary of cookies because they can be abused. This is not because they give access to information on your computer but because they can reveal your surfing behavior. Veen (2001) gives the example of advertising service provider Doubleclick, which can track people's visits to sites that use their service and build a profile. This definitely seems like an invasion of privacy. Some users, however, are tolerant of this.

You should also provide a way for the user to verify the identity of a secure site. Use a padlock icon as a link the display of your verification service's credentials.

Therefore   **Take security seriously, but take care not to frighten users with unnecessary warnings.**

~ ~ ~

This pattern conceals a massively complex subject that may need a pattern language in its own right. Since we are only concerned with security issues that impact upon usability, we can safely halt the discussion here. However, make sure you do not go too far and indulge in *PARANOID SECURITY* (74).

昗73   Oblique landmarks

AKA   **PARTIAL LINE OF SIGHT**, **DISABLED IRRELEVANT THINGS** (Tidwell)

You understand **WYSIWYCU (70)** and the need for users to **GO BACK TO A SAFE PLACE (34)**.

~ ~ ~

Problem   **How do you draw attention to features of your site that are only usable indirectly or when the user is in a certain state?**

There is a theory in architecture known as space syntax (Hillier, 1996), which says that the geometry of spaces affects our reaction to them and thus the way they are used and their usability. Hillier argues that user-friendly cities are those where landmarks are always approached tangentially rather than head-on. Also, landmarks are often partially visible from some distance. He gives the City of London as one example of an urban area with these properties and Manhattan as its antithesis. Interestingly, the City was not planned and Manhattan was. However, you navigate the Manhattan grid successfully by understanding the way the streets are numbered. In the City, you don't even need to know the names of the roads. Our contention here is that user interfaces should be more like the City than Manhattan.

In conventional GUI design, this kind of property is often achieved by greying out menu items that are not currently available but could become so in some future state, giving the user something just visible to work towards.

You can't easily use 'greying out' in current browsers, although some kind of color-change convention is a possibility. The way you name links can also be important. Another way to let people see what is just round the corner is a good site map or navigation bar. Important pages are the public buildings of your site; highlight them in some way. In the image above, notice how it is clear from its façade that the porticoed building is important in some way: perhaps a museum, basilica or opera house.

When you open a new browser window, make this obvious by off-setting it slightly compared with the window that is currently open. In this way, the user can see there is a landmark to head back to.

Therefore   **Provide visual and textual cues to show users what is available on the site. Make it clear what the 'public buildings' are.**

~ ~ ~

This pattern is terminal within this language.

昊 74   *Paranoid security*

AKA   **BIG BROTHER**

Image reproduced courtesy of Dorling Kindersley and by kind permission of the Trustees of the Imperial War Museum, London

Naturally, you are concerned about **SECURITY AND ENCRYPTION (72)**. You have **CLASSIFIED YOUR SITE (11)**.

~ ~ ~

Problem

Companies want to be sure that their customers are who they say they are. Customers want privacy and find elaborate dialogs irritating. How can these forces be balanced? How do you authenticate a visitor without trampling on their privacy?

The amount of security that a site requires varies according to the business of the site. An appropriate analogy is the security of buildings. Banks are usually harder to break into than carpet warehouses. Homes containing valuables are often protected better than the homes of poor people. People trade off the cost of burglar alarms and barred windows against the cost of recovery strategies like household insurance. In some districts, even poor people have to protect their homes against the risk of violence and malicious damage.

In the context of the web, there is a range of types of site with varying security needs. At one extreme there hobby sites that are unlikely to be hacked and on which there is really nothing to steal. One level up from this, we might consider an academic's site containing résumés and publications. The academic would be unhappy if someone downloaded a paper and altered it or claimed to have written it. In fact, recently there have been mutterings in academe about students populating their essays with words in this way. The common solution is to publish material in some uneditable format such as PDF.

Commercial sites need to take more care. The user should be able to verify that the site is really the one it claims to be before entering credit card details. The common solution is to use a trusted third party such as Verisign to provide this confidence. Commercial transactions may need to be encrypted. Banking sites have even stronger requirements.

Problems only arise when the degree of security outweighs the need for it. Enforced registration or authentication dialogs will deter the casual (but harmless) browser and may cost sales. Messages that highlight the risks to the user can frighten people away too easily. Only display warnings when they tell the user something that they really need to know.

Example

The author's trireme.com e-mails are visible to some of his colleagues. He therefore wants purchase confirmations to go to his private e-mail address (which he accesses using a non-web-aware program). When he tries to buy from some sites having logged on as ian@trireme.com, he is asked to type his address. He enters his other (CompuServe) address. The site rejects his form. They lose his business. Amazon lets him do this, so why can't this site? It's pure paranoia.

Therefore   **Base security measures on a thorough risk analysis. Relate security measures to your business objectives. Trade off security measures against well-thought-out recovery procedures – and don't forget that the best security can be bypassed by the determined. Only use authentication techniques when it is absolutely necessary. Don't frighten users with unnecessary warnings.**

$$\sim \ \sim \ \sim$$

This antipattern is terminal within this language.

75 Sense of location in workflow

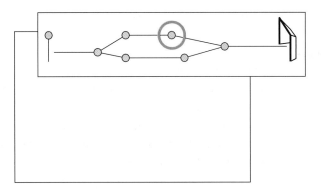

You have **ESTABLISHED THE USE CASES (3)** and **CLASSIFIED YOUR SITE (11)** and found that it is a workflow site. You know about the need to provide **A SENSE OF LOCATION (15)** and a **SENSE OF PROGRESS (48)**.

~ ~ ~

Problem

How do you let a user know where they are during a transaction? How do you indicate the progress they are making towards their goal?

Users need and want to know where they are during a task. This is especially important on workflow sites because doing things in the wrong order can wreak havoc on transactions.

You need to make it clear where the user is in relation to a transaction and be forgiving of errors. What is in the shopping basket? How can I change it? Tidwell's **EDITABLE COLLECTION** advises that you show such collections to the user with clear methods for removing and changing items.

Example

A user of tesco.com, a supermarket that decided to sell insurance products, reports the following experience (*Computing*, 2001/06/28). He looked at the site and found the quoted price attractive. Therefore he decided to buy. When no policy arrived for some time, he contacted his credit card company only to find that no payment had been made. Tesco had no record of the transaction. The reason for this was that the user had not saved the quotation before moving on to the purchase. As a result, the user had been driving illegally for over a week. Two things are wrong here. First, a logically unnecessary step is enforced, leading to confusion. Second – and this is a very common experience – the site allowed the user to fill in a form without providing help on the workflow. It then threw away the result without telling the user what it had done. This pattern is related to Tidwell's **INTERACTION HISTORY**.

Therefore

Always include Next **and** Previous **buttons that relate to the workflow. Don't rely on the browser back and forward buttons alone. Use BREADCRUMBS (23). Draw a task map as above, showing where the user is in the process. Test all possible paths through transactions, not just the ones you would like users to follow. Provide confirmations as each transaction succeeds or fails.**

~ ~ ~

Use **BREADCRUMBS (23)** and remember that **CONTENT IS LINKED TO NAVIGATION (76)**.

Contributors and sources

Richard Dué.
Detlef Vollmann.

吴 76   Content is linked to navigation ★

You are concerned with providing a **SENSE OF LOCATION IN WORK-FLOW (75)** through a sound navigation scheme, but your development budget is limited.

~ ~ ~

Problem

Can I base the navigation scheme on a standard product and so save development time?

The study by Spool *et al.* (1999) showed that when users visited shell sites, they found it very hard to hard to search for the information they needed. Shell sites are those where a fixed organization and navigation scheme is defined and content is then plugged into it.

Just as form and content are intertwined in art and nature, so on the web. The way you navigate depends deeply on the material you are navigating, and therefore the navigation scheme should reflect the exigencies of the content as well as the use cases.

Consider, for example, the different ways that bibliographical, leisure and commercial sites are approached. A tourist arrives at a travel site with a conception of library-style organization that he might have used in his day job – a librarian.

On workflow sites, it is clear that the workflow itself should guide at least some of the navigation.

Therefore

Link navigation to a model of users' domain knowledge. One page implements one workflow step. Avoid shell architecture.

~ ~ ~

This pattern is terminal within this language.

Contributors and sources

Richard Dué.
Detlef Vollmann.
Spool *et al.* (1999).

昊 77   Button gravity ★

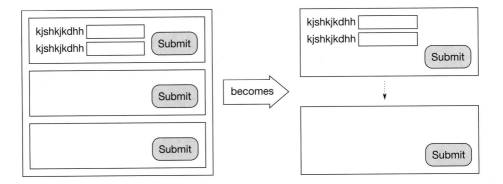

You are trying to avoid having too many pages displayed within a task, process or use case. You have therefore **ESTABLISHED THE USE CASES (3)** and want to give the user a **SENSE OF LOCATION IN WORKFLOW (75)**.

~ ~ ~

Problem

Users usually scroll down to the bottom of the page, ignoring other buttons. You need to make sure they do not miss important ones.

The study by Spool *et al.* (1999) showed that users missed buttons that were not at the bottom of pages. Their attention fell naturally to the bottom of the page.

To avoid this, we can either insist on one button per page or make sure there are clear visual clues as to what the buttons are for and plenty of feedback when they are clicked. You might consider validating the sequence of clicks before submitting the page.

Examples
Filling in an application form.
Confirming a purchase.

Therefore

Design pages so that there is a single Submit button at the bottom of each page. It should be to the right of the displayed area (not the whole of a wide page). If you duplicate this button higher up, then make sure it appears above the fold, even on small screens.

~ ~ ~

PIPELINE INTERACTION (78).

Contributors
and sources

Paul Dyson.
Dave Sissons.
Spool *et al.*(1999).

昊 78   Pipeline interaction

Image courtesy of
www.ads-pipe.com

You are trying to give a **SENSE OF PROGRESS (48)** and are aware of
the phenomenon of **BUTTON GRAVITY (77)**.

~ ~ ~

Problem

Sometimes, a process-driven interaction can constrain user
choices and behavior ('constrain' because pipeline interaction
may never be the ideal solution). Business procedures demand
that information is displayed or captured in a certain order. This
order may not suit the user or conform to their mental model of
the domain.

As Hegel put it, freedom is the recognition of necessity. Users
should be free to do things their way unless they are engaged in a
dialog with your business processes that might harm one of the
parties if they fail to follow the necessary steps. They will ultimately feel less free when their transaction fails and the wrong
goods arrive.

Examples

Insurance quotations (Royal and Sun Alliance). The site was written on top of an existing system, so the developers were constrained by the way that system worked. For example, they needed to identify who the customer was and the car that they would be driving before taking details of who else would be driving it. They were therefore forced to ask for information in a certain order.

The shopping basket at lastminute.com provides another typical solution.

Therefore

Provide a series of linked pages that the user must visit in strict sequence. Use SENSE OF PROGRESS (48) to ensure that commitment points are made plain.

Allow users to revisit previous pages and correct them. Cache information entered in case of line failure. Don't force people to enter stuff that isn't essential (e.g. their fax numbers) or in fixed categories (e.g. UK instead of Wales)

~ ~ ~

This pattern is terminal within this language.

Contributors and sources

Paul Dyson.
Dave Sissons.

79   Display the options

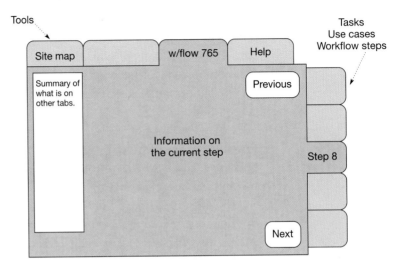

You have **ESTABLISHED THE USE CASES (3)** and **CLASSIFIED YOUR SITE (11).**You understand **THE RHETORIC OF ARRIVAL AND DEPARTURE (20).**

~ ~ ~

Problem

What is the best way to show the users how to use the site and what options are available?

Navigation bars and search engines provide the basic option display but are limited when the site is complex. One way to show options is to use a tab-card layout, such as the one above. Tab-card metaphors can be useful on all sites, but they are especially so on workflow sites.

Tabs must be drawn in such a way that it is clear which one is active (in front). You may use color to achieve this aim, making the color of the active tab the same as the active area or the **NAVIGATION BAR (25)** below the tab. A tab bar should be a single graphic so that it loads quickly. **THE RHETORIC AND ARRIVAL AND DEPARTURE (20)** suggests that you should provide pop-ups or 'roll- overs' to show where the tab will lead. If you do this by making each tab a graphic, then the result will be both slow and messy (*cf.* Krug, 2000).

Amazon adopts this approach well. However, as their site content has grown, the tab organization has become less effective.

Therefore

Use tabs only when there are fewer than about eight options. Consider a see-through tab card that summarizes the information on the other cards. On workflow sites, provide 'buttony' Previous **and** Next **buttons. Ensure that the site logo, navigation and tabs load quickly**

~ ~ ~

This pattern is terminal within this language.

Contributors and sources

Richard Dué.
Detlef Vollmann.

**Oh! And by
the way...**

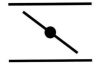

That icon! For those who could not guess the meaning of the icon in Pattern 57, it represents the choke of a mid-twentieth-century car. Recognizing it as such depends either entirely on memory or on the knowledge that a carburettor contains within it a 'butterfly': a device consisting of a flat metal plate that pivots about an axial pin to allow more or less air into the combustion process. Once you know this, the meaning is obvious. If you don't have this fundamental engineering knowledge, you have to remember the meaning. This means that most readers under 40 will not have understood the meaning of this symbol.

4

Examples of using the *wu* language

Example is the school of mankind, and they will learn at no other.
Edmund Burke, *Two Letters on the Proposals for Peace with the Regicide Directory*

This chapter is designed to illustrate how you might use the *wu* language or create specialized sublanguages out of it.

4.1 Designing a workflow-centric site

Richard Dué and Detlef Vollmann constructed the following subset of the *wu* patterns to capture how a designer might go about constructing a workflow site. These are the essential patterns to think about when starting on the design of such a site:

1   **ESTABLISH THE BUSINESS OBJECTIVES (1).**

2   **BUSINESS PROCESS MODEL (2).**

3   **ESTABLISH THE USE CASES (3)** derived from the business process model.

4   **CLASSIFY YOUR SITE (11).** If it fits the workflow pattern, then

5   **USER-CENTERD SITE STRUCTURE (13)** with tasks defined by the established use cases.

6   **CREATE A SITE MAP (12)** showing all the workflows (again based on the established use cases) and objects in the type model.

7 Provide **CONTEXT-SENSITIVE HELP (17)** based on the site map and all the workflows and upon the established use cases.

8 Provide a **SENSE OF LOCATION IN WORKFLOW (75)**.

9 **DISPLAY THE OPTIONS (79)** using a scheme connected to the help button.

10 Create a 'contact us' button using **CONTEXT-SENSITIVE CONTACT LINK (33)**, adding **THE HUMAN TOUCH (30)**.

11 Don't forget to think about the **BACK BUTTON (35)**.

12 Ensure that **CONTENT IS LINKED TO NAVIGATION (76)** by using one page per workflow.

13 Make sure your site can still provide a **SENSE OF LOCATION IN WORKFLOW (75)**.

14 Apply **SYMMETRY AND IDEMPOTENCY (22)**.

15 Apply **AESTHETICS (16)**.

At this point, one would consider whether any of the abstract patterns were applicable and use various navigation patterns, depending on the actual content of the site and the use cases identified.

Other more detailed patterns would be applied depending on factors such as organizational ethos and site content and purpose. Such considerations would generate a site-specific sublanguage.

4.2   Designing the *wu* site

In Section 4.1, we described an abstract, high-level subset of *wu*. In this section, we examine the thought process behind the construction of an actual, concrete site: the *wu* website itself. We will consider many patterns in the language and for each one consider:

◆ whether it is relevant;

◆ why it can be ignored;

◆ how it applies;

◆ what solution it generates.

The reader will notice that none of the workflow patterns have been used. It will also be noticed that compromises have been made due to time and budget pressures. This will mean that the *wu* website will not be perfect. While even commercial sites with huge development budgets remain less than perfect, we think this is understandable and excusable – even for a site concerned with web design.

1 ESTABLISH THE BUSINESS OBJECTIVES

Every website should use this pattern. But this is easy in this case. The site is there to support readers of the book and provide a version of the language that is easy to navigate, exploring the connections between patterns. There is an overriding requirement to work with a low budget in terms of both cost and time. Because of this, we will have to work with only the crudest of web-authoring tools. The site we are working at has no licence for Dreamweaver or the like. We identify a risk: can we do this entirely with Word?

2 BUSINESS PROCESS MODEL

There is no business to model, so we reject this pattern.

3 ESTABLISH THE USE CASES

There seem to be four:

- Find out about the *wu* language, what it is, who created it, how to use it.

- Access the patterns.

- Navigate around the language.

- Link to related sites.

4 TIMEBOXES

This is a controlling pattern in this project. The site must be ready by the time the book is published.

5 GRADUAL STIFFENING

The site will continue to evolve based on experience and feedback.

6 AUTOMATED TESTING

The low budget precludes the use of such tools.

7 USABILITY TESTING

The low budget precludes the use of formal sessions, but the site will continue to evolve based on feedback.

8 GET-IT?

Friends and family will be used.

9 RETEST WHEN CONTENT UPDATED

Of course!

10 TWO-YEAR-OLD BROWSER

This may be tricky considering the low budget and the primitive authoring tools in use. The intention is to make the site work on IE and Netscape.

11 CLASSIFY YOUR SITE

It's an information site and stateless. It could be regarded as a typical exploration site.

12 SITE MAP

The diagrams in Chapter 3 were the basis of this.

13 USER-CENTERD SITE STRUCTURE

Not applicable. The content is the chief determinant of structure.

14 SEARCH BOX

This is not applicable because we want people to buy the book as well and use its index for this kind of use. Also, the budget has restricted us in this respect.

15 SENSE OF LOCATION

Use a pointer in the navigation scheme and display pattern names as page headers.

16 AESTHETICS

We will do our best.

17 CONTEXT-SENSITIVE HELP

Not applicable. What you see is what you get.

20 THE RHETORIC OF ARRIVAL AND DEPARTURE

This is managed by the site map and the links to related patterns.

22 SYMMETRY AND IDEMPOTENCY

The links to related patterns should be symmetrical. We expect some errors in this respect to show up in testing.

23 BREADCRUMBS

We will not use these because the use cases do not indicate a need to navigate in this way.

24 SITE LOGO AT TOP LEFT

We use the Chinese character for the *wu* language.

25 NAVIGATION BAR

It must be at the top of the page, to the right of the *wu* icon.

26 THREE-REGION LAYOUT

KISS says we can do it with just two because of the site map organization.

27 NO FRAMES ON PUBLIC SITES

We will not use frames.

28 HOME PAGE

29 TRITE FONTS

Since we are developing in an MS environment, we will use only Arial and Times New Roman. This should cover most users. In a later timebox, we plan to put in font substitution code.

30 THE HUMAN TOUCH

It's littered throughout the site.

31 LINKS TO MANY SITES

There is a page of links to related sites. To avoid copyright restrictions, we will link to the pages used for sensitizing images. This means that we cannot predict that they will be the same as they were when the book was produced, but it seems a fair trade-off on a non-commercial site such as this.

34 GO BACK TO A SAFE PLACE

The *wu* icon should take you back to the diagram that you reached the pattern from unless it appears in two diagrams, in which case you go back to the diagram selector page. If you are not on a pattern, you get back to the home page. This is a complicated scheme but it seems to work.

35 BACK BUTTON

Leave the browser to do the work here. But we need to test that you can get back when we link to other sites.

42 DOWNLOAD TIME

The slowest part of each page will be the sensitizing image. We will put these in separate pages and make them optional, with text describing what they are.

43 DESIGN PAGES FOR SCANNING

We highlight the problem and solution in a different colour.

44 SHORT TEXTS

We will break up the content so that there is one page per pattern. Perhaps we should go further and display only the problem, solution and links, making the body of the pattern optional to view. Gradual stiffening says do this later.

45 ANCHORS AWAY

Version 0.1 of the site had anchors, but it took aeons to download. We must get rid of them.

47 SEPARATE PRINT PAGES

This is for a later timebox.

51 THE HALT AND THE LAME AND THE STRANGER AT THE DOOR

This is for a later timebox.

52 INTERNATIONALIZATION

This is for a later timebox.

55 CONTENT BEFORE GRAPHICS

Download the pattern and make the images optional.

56 NATURAL METAPHORS

The leading metaphors are Alexander's patterns and the idea of a network of patterns shown graphically by the site map.

57 WORDS BEFORE ICONS

There should be no icons.

58 WHITE SPACE SEPARATES CONTENT

Use colour to delineate text segments.

59 BROKEN BUTTONS

Apart from the navigation bar, there should be no buttons other than the site map images and links to other sites. Put links on a separate line.

60 MAGIC MARGINS

This is for a later timebox.

62 UNIQUE NAMES FOR PAGES, TITLES AND META-TAGS

Use the pattern names for page names.

64 STORE CONTENT IN A DATABASE

This facility is not available.

76 CONTENT IS LINKED TO NAVIGATION

See the site map.

79 DISPLAY THE OPTIONS

This is achieved via the navigation bar.

4.3 Designing and improving other kinds of site

The approach to other site types will be similar. Go through the patterns in numerical order asking yourself the same questions:

- Is it is relevant?
- Can it be ignored?
- How does it apply in this case?
- What solution will it generate?

Next, go through the patterns you have not eliminated, starting always with pattern number 1. Follow the links in the resultant context sections. For each pattern you reach, ask the same questions again and make sure you have considered each pattern in the opening context.

For a team development, convert your conclusions into tasks, perhaps using Kent Beck's idea of task cards (Beck, 2000). Each task should take only a few days to implement. Write tests for the tasks.

In the case of an existing site, ask also how it supports or violates each pattern. Then follow the same procedure to specify its redesign.

The author would be interested to know whether your site improves as a result and whether you have discovered any new patterns in the process or found flaws (of which there must be many) in the patterns in this book. You can contact him at ian@trireme.com.

APPENDIX

wu patterns in brief

The *wu* patterns are listed here in numerical order. The page reference is given after the pattern name and star rating. Any aliases for each pattern are listed below its name.

References and bibliography

Alexander, C. (1964) *Notes on the Synthesis of Form*, Harvard: Harvard University Press

Alexander, C. (1979) *The Timeless Way of Building*, Oxford: Oxford University Press

Alexander, C. (1996) *A Foreshadowing of 21st Century Art*, New York: Oxford University Press

Alexander, C. (1999) The origins of pattern theory: the future of the theory and the generation of a living world, *IEEE Software* September/October, 71–82

Alexander, C., Ishikawa, S. and Silverstein, M. (1977) *A Pattern Language*, Oxford: Oxford University Press

Allen, P. and Frost, S. (1998) *Component-Based Development for Enterprise Systems: applying the SELECT perspective*, Cambridge: Cambridge University Press/SIGS

Alpert, S., Brown, K. and Woolf, B.R. (1998) *The Design Patterns Smalltalk Companion*, Reading MA: Addison-Wesley

Apple Computer Inc. (1987) *Apple Human Interface Guidelines: the apple desktop interface*, Cupertino, CA: Addison-Wesley

Austin, J.L. (1962) *How to Do Things with Words*, Cambridge MA: Harvard University Press

Baecker, R.M. and Buxton, W.A.S. (eds) (1987) *Readings in Human Computer Interaction: a multi-disciplinary approach*, San Mateo CA: Morgan Kaufmann

Barfield, L. (1993) *The User Interface: concepts and design*, Wokingham: Addison-Wesley

Beck, K. (1997) *Smalltalk Best Practice Patterns*, Upper Saddle River NJ: Prentice Hall

Beck, K. (2000) *Extreme Programming Explained: embrace change*, Reading MA: Addison-Wesley.

Borchers, J. (2001) *A Pattern Approach to Interaction Design*, Chichester, Wiley

Borenstein, N.S. (1991) *Programming as if People Mattered: friendly programs, software engineering, and other noble delusions*, Princeton NJ: Princeton University Press

Brown, J.S. and Duguid, P. (1996) Keeping it Simple, in Winograd, T. (ed), *Bringing Design to Software*, New York: ACM Press

Burns, J. (2001) *Web Site Design Goodies*, New York: Que

Buschmann, F., Meunier, R., Rohnert, H., Sommerlad, P. and Stal, M. (1996) *Pattern-oriented Software Architecture: a system of patterns*, Chichester, Wiley

Cato, J. (2001) *User Centred Interface Design*, Harlow: Addison-Wesley

Cheesman, J. and Daniels, J. (2000) *UML Components*, Harlow: Addison-Wesley

Coad, P. (1992) *Object-Oriented Patterns, Comms. ACM* **35**(9), 152–58

Coad, P., North, D. and Mayfield, M. (1997) *Object Models: strategies, patterns and applications*, Upper Saddle River NJ: Prentice Hall

Coad, P., LeFebvre, E. and DeLuca, J. (1999) *Java Modeling in Color with UML*, Upper Saddle River NJ: Prentice Hall

Cockburn, A. (2000) *Writing Effective Use Cases*, Reading MA: Addison-Wesley

Constantine, L.L. and Lockwood, L. (1999) *Software for Use: models and methods of usage-centred design*, Reading MA: Addison-Wesley

Cooper, A. (1995) *About Face: the essentials of user interface design*, Foster City CA: IDG Books Worldwide

Cooper, A. (1999) *The Inmates are Running the Asylum*, New York: SAMS

Cooper, J.W. (2000) *Java Design Patterns*, Reading MA: Addison-Wesley

Coplien, J.O. (1992) *Advanced C++: programming styles and idioms*, Reading MA: Addison-Wesley

Coplien, J.O. (1995) A generative development-process pattern language, in Coplien, J.O. and Schmidt, D. (eds) *Pattern Languages of Program Design*, Reading MA: Addison-Wesley

Coplien, J. O. (1999) Reevaluating the architectural metaphor: toward piecemeal growth, *IEEE Software* September/October, 40–4.

Coplien, J.O. and Schmidt, D. (eds) (1995) *Pattern Languages of Program Design*, Reading MA: Addison-Wesley

Donnelly, V. (2000) *Designing Easy-to-use Websites*, Reading MA: Addison-Wesley

D'Souza, D.F. and Wills, A.C. (1999) *Objects, Components and Frameworks with UML: the catalysis approach*, Reading MA: Addison-Wesley

Flores, F. (1997) The leaders of the future, in Denning, P.J. and Metcalfe, R.M. (eds) *Beyond Calculation: the next 50 years of computing*, New York: Copernicus

Fowler, M. (1996) *Analysis Patterns*, Harlow: Addison-Wesley

Fowler, M. (1997) *UML Distilled*, 2nd edn, Harlow: Addison-Wesley

Fowler, M. (1999) *Refactoring: improving the design of existing code*, Reading MA: Addison-Wesley

Gabriel, R.P (1996) *Patterns of Software*, Oxford: Oxford University Press

Galitz, W. (1981) *Human Factors in Office Automation*, Atlanta, GA: Life Office Management Association

Gamma, E., Helm, R. Johnson, R. and Vlissedes, J. (1995) *Design Patterns: elements of reusable object-oriented software*, Reading MA: Addison-Wesley

Graham, I. (1995) *Migrating to Object Technology*, Wokingham: Addison-Wesley

Graham, I. (2001) *Object-Oriented Methods: principles and practice*, 3rd edn, Harlow: Addison-Wesley

Graham, I. (2002) Fair web usability patterns from the *wu* language, *Proc. EuroPlop '02*, UVK Universitätsverlag Konstanz

Graham, I.M. (1994) On the Impossibility of Artificial Intelligence, *BCS Specialist Group in Expert Systems Newsletter*, Summer 1994

Grand, M. (1998) *Patterns in Java – Volume 1*, New York: Wiley

Guidice, A. and Dennis, M. (2001) *Web Design Essentials*, New York: Adobe Press

Hillier, W. (1996) *Space is the Machine*, Cambridge: Cambridge University Press

IBM (1992) *Object-Oriented Interface Design: CUA guidelines*, New York: QUE

Jackson, M.A. (1998) A Discipline of Description, *Requirements Engineering* 3(2), 73–8

Jacobson, I., Ericsson, M. and Jacobson, A. (1995) *The Object Advantage: business process re-engineering with object technology*, Wokingham: Addison-Wesley

Johnson, P. (1992) *Human Computer Interaction: psychology, task analysis and software engineering*, London: McGraw-Hill

Koch, N. and Rossi, G. (2002) Patterns for Adaptive Personalized Web Applications, *Proc. EuroPLoP '02*, UVK Universitätsverlag Konstanz

Kruchten, P. (1999) *The Rational Unified Process*, Reading MA: Addison-Wesley

Krug, S. (2000) *Don't Make Me Think, A Common Sense Approach to Web Usability*, Indianapolis, IN: New Riders

Kwa'ioloa, M. and Burt, B. (1997) *Living Tradition*, London: British Museum Press

Laurel, B. (ed.) (1990) *The Art of Computer Interface Design*, Reading, MA: Addison-Wesley

Lee, G. (1993) *Object-Oriented GUI Application Development*, Englewood Cliffs, NJ: Prentice Hall

Lindgaard, G. (1994) *Usability Testing and System Evaluation*, London: Stanley Thomas

Lyardet, F. and Rossi, G. (2001) Web Usability Patterns, *Proc. EuroPLop '01*, UVK Universitätsverlag Konstanz

Maiden, N.A.M., Cisse, M., Perez, H. and Manuel, D. (1998) *CREWS Validation Frames: Patterns for Validating Systems Requirements*, London: Centre for Human Computer Interface Design, City University

Martin, J. and Odell, J.J. (1998) *Object-Oriented Methods: A Foundation (UML Edition)*, Englewood Cliffs NJ: Prentice Hall

Microsoft (1992) *The Windows Interface: an application design guide*, Seattle: Microsoft Corp.

Miller, G.A. (1956) The magical number seven, plus or minus two: some limits on out capacity for processing information. *Psychological Review* 63, 81–97

Navarro, A. (2001) *Effective Web Design*, New York: Sybex International

NeXT Computers Inc. (1992) *NeXTSTEP User Interface Guidelines: Release 3*, Reading MA: Addison-Wesley

Nielson, J. (2000) *Designing Web Usability*; Indianapolis: New Riders

Nielson, J. and Tahir, M. (2002) *Homepage Usability*, Indianapolis: New Riders

Norman, D. (1988) *The Design of Everyday Things*, New York: Basic Books

O'Callaghan, A. (1997a) *Object-oriented reverse engineering, Application Development Adviser* **1**(1), 35–9

O'Callaghan, A. (1997b) Realizing the reality, *Application Development Adviser* **1**(2), 30–3

O'Callaghan, A. (1998) A plethora of patterns, *Application Development Adviser* **1**(3), 32–3

O'Callaghan, A.J. (2000) Patterns for an Architectural Praxis, *Proceedings of the European Pattern Languages of Program Design*, Irsee, Germany

Pawson, R. (2002) *Naked Objects*, Harlow: Addison-Wesley

Redmond-Pyle, D. and Moore, A. (1995) *Graphical User Interface Design and Evaluation: a practical process*, London: Prentice Hall

Rising, L. (ed.) (1998) *The Patterns Handbook*, New York: Cambridge University Press.

Schneiderman, B. (1987) *Designing the User Interface: strategies for effective human computer interaction*, Reading MA: Addison-Wesley

Searle, J. R. (1969) *Speech Acts*, Cambridge: Cambridge University Press

Spool, J., Scanlon, T., Schroeder, W., Snyder, C. and DeAngelo, T. (1999) *Web Site Usability: a designer's guide*, San Francisco CA: Morgan Kaufmann

Stapleton, J. (1997) *Dynamic Systems Development Method: the method in practice*, Harlow: Addison-Wesley

Stephenson, N. (1992) *Snow Crash*, London: Roc

Suchman, L.A. (1987) *Plans and Situated Actions: the problem of human machine communication*, Cambridge: Cambridge University Press

Thimbleby, H. (1990) *User Interface Design*, New York: ACM Press (Addison-Wesley)

Tognazzini, B. (1992) *TOG on Interface*, Reading MA: Addison-Wesley

Tufte, E.R. (1983) *The Visual Display of Quantitative Information*, New York: Graphics Press

Tufte, E.R. (1990) *Envisioning Information*, New York: Graphics Press

Valqui K., Freire E. (2001) *Web Design and Development*, New York: Charles River Media

Van Duyne, D.K., Landay, J. and Hong, J.I. (2002) *The Design of Sites*, Reading MA: Addison-Wesley

Veen J. (2001) *The Art and Science of Web Design*, Indianapolis: New Riders

Winograd, T. and Flores, F. (1986) *Understanding Computers and Cognition*, Reading MA: Addison-Wesley

Name index

Subject index

All patterns are in **SMALL CAPITALS**; *wu* patterns have a pattern number after them. A *BOLD* page number signifies the page where a *wu* pattern is described.

Inst
the most e
p

Safari Tech Books Online is a
access to highly relevant, technically a
books. Safari provides access to information
programmers and administrators in today's dynam

Search for exactly what you
when you need it.

Simultaneous search of all the latest IT books

Safari contains the latest and most innovative titles from well-known and leading IT publishers such as:

- Addison-Wesley ● Adobe Press ● Cisco Press ● New Riders
- Peachpit Press ● Prentice Hall PTR ● Que ● SAMS ● O'Reilly

Specific search capabilities

The Safari search engine gives you relevance-ranked results in a matter of seconds. The titles and chapters most likely to answer your questions are listed first, saving you valuable time.

Cut and paste code

Safari allows you to cut and paste code to save time and eliminate typographical errors.

Up to 100 new titles added to the site each month

Each month up to 100 new titles covering a variety of topics are added to the site and every month you have the option to swap your chosen books for new titles.

FOR YOUR FREE TRIAL

Email: **safari@pearsoned-ema.com**
Or visit: **www.it-minds.com/goto/safari**